THE
PREACHER'S PAPERBACK
LIBRARY

The Preacher's Paperback Library
Edmund A. Steimle, Consulting Editor

Violent Sleep

*Notes Toward the
Development of Sermons
for the Modern City*

RICHARD LUECKE

FORTRESS PRESS • PHILADELPHIA

ABOUT THE
PREACHER'S PAPERBACK LIBRARY

The renewal of the church in our time has touched many aspects of parish life: liturgy and sacraments, biblical and theological concern, the place of the laity, work with small groups. But little has been said or done with regard to the renewal of the church in the pulpit.

The Preacher's Paperback Library is offered in the hope that it will contribute to the renewal of the preaching ministry. It will not stoop to providing "sermon starters" or other homiletical gimmicks. It will, rather, attempt to hold in balance the emphasis which contemporary theologians and biblical scholars lay upon the centrality of proclamation and the very practical concerns of theological students and parish pastors who are engaged in the demanding task of preparing sermons of biblical and theological depth which also speak to the contemporary world.

To that end, the series will provide reprints of fundamental homiletical studies not presently available and contemporary studies in areas of immediate concern to the preacher. Moreover, because the study of sermons themselves can be of invaluable help in every aspect of the preparation of the sermon, volumes of sermons with introductory notes will appear from time to time. The sermons will include reprints of outstanding preachers in the past as well as sermons by contemporary preachers who have given evidence both of depth and of imaginative gifts in communication. It is our hope that each volume in The Preacher's Paperback Library, prepared with the specific task of sermon preparation in mind, will contribute to the renewal of the preaching ministry.

In *Violent Sleep* Richard Luecke has provided a rare and invaluable contribution to the work of the preacher. As its subtitle indicates, the book lies somewhere between the scholarly commentaries and finished sermons. The research which goes into exegesis is evident throughout and the implications of the exegesis for the contemporary thrust of the text are sketched in with broad strokes of depth and perception. Thus the book avoids the superficiality of homiletical deceptions and allows no reader to "lift" a sermon from the finished product.

The student of preaching will find two specific aids in this work. First, there is obvious help in the interpretation of the texts under examination: the prophecy of Jonah, the Matthew narrative of the temptation in the wilderness, three incidents associated with the Passion and Easter. This volume deserves to be used along with other commentaries related to these specific passages. Second, the student will also find here a model for a crucial stage in the preparation of sermons: the use of the text to give insight concerning the contemporary scene. The reader will not soon forget the incisive treatment of "sleep" and the "bloody city."

What remains, of course, as the author points out, is that "the details and colors need to be supplied" and the specific target needs to be specified. The value of *Violent Sleep* lies in the excitement it brings to the imagination of the preacher, but it does not take the joy out of the creative work still to be accomplished by the imagination newly aroused.

EDMUND A. STEIMLE

Union Theological Seminary
New York, New York
The Circumcision and Name of Jesus, 1969

viii

FOREWORD

"Never write a preface, never give an interview" was the advice of James Joyce to Samuel Beckett. Of course, they were talking about finished artistic products, which are peculiarly unique and in an important sense not discussable. But something similar could be said, in spite of all the coffee-hour discussions, about finished sermons.

Traditionally, the sermon was followed by the Offertory and Communion, or prayer and dismissal, and not by more talk nor even dialogue. The sermon was thought to represent a decisive expression which related the hearer on the basis of his faith to the realities of his own time and place. The only appropriate response was to get on with the song or the action prescribed. Our difficulty with that, perhaps, stems from the fact that we have lost any such expectation for words, or have had little experience with words which bring us down to earth in that way, or both. But all artistic attempts do not succeed either; Giacometti once explained his steady stream of works by saying that he kept trying to find out why he had failed. Preaching goes on too, in spite of misgivings on every side; the important thing, perhaps, is to remember *what* is being tried.

Since what follows in this book is neither art nor finished sermons, some explanations should be offered. We might call them "sermonic essays," though that phrase borders on a self-contradiction and should be discarded after first use by anyone who is serious about words. These chapters offer no more than "notes toward" the development of sermons, even though those notes are set down in the shape and even the tone of traditional sermons. Let us agree that these chapters are meant to be helpful to people still practicing the sermonic art.

Specifically, they are meant to be helpful during Lent, when a little hitchhiking along the way from text to utterance is welcomed by people who have to do a lot of the latter. There are ten essays in all, seven for the weeks of Lent and three for Holy Week. They do not comprise a single "series"; that might run an even greater risk of becoming contrived or tedious. Yet some sustained treatment of continuous texts is desirable during these weeks of intensified discipline. That includes both patient reading (not merely "raiding") of the Scriptures and a persistent attempt to follow through to present proclamations (a requirement often displaced by needed, happily time-consuming, expositions of a text). Thus, three of our pre-sermons are on the Book of Jonah, four on the Lenten Gospel of the temptations of Jesus, and three on the scenes remembered on Maundy Thursday, Good Friday, and Easter Sunday. A focus of all ten is found in a single picture from the passion story which seems particularly suited to the day—the sleep of the disciples.

Since that picture is used throughout, it seems important to make some qualifications with respect to it. One hopes, in retrospect, that these chapters have not been unduly severe with the disciples. To be sure, the Gospels themselves take their raps at the disciples—no doubt, for methodic reasons. But if we make caricatures of the disciples before the crucifixion and heroes of them afterwards, we run the risk of losing the very point the Gospels were trying to make. Holden Caulfield was probably too easily offended by the disciples for his own good: to him they seemed chosen "at random" —as though a more select group might have done better or would surely do better now. But the disciples were befuddled in the Gospels for the sake of something which was waiting to be discovered; and no doubt they continued to be, to some degree, "foolish men, and slow of heart to believe" even after the waking of Easter. It is not as though they switched, once and for all, from obtuse unbelief to sheer faith. They went "from faith to faith." So does every man alive.

Some initial explanations should be set down concerning the manner of moving from text to newer utterance in these essays. None of the texts treated here can simply be repeated in the expectation that it will communicate its original meaning, or very much new meaning either. The conceptions of "water" in the song of Jonah, "wilderness" in Matthew, and "king" or "light" in the Fourth Gospel are samples of understandings formed in cultural settings very different from our own. Insofar as the issues addressed in these texts are still present, they appear in different terms and in different practical engagements. Nor can interpretations be abstracted from these texts and then be repeated or applied without restatement in every new situation. Any such abstraction, even of "eternal truths" or of constantly needed distinctions, is itself historical in the terms it uses and the targets it addresses. Even palpable hits (and all these texts as well as many subsequent doctrines were presumably that) do not eliminate the need to take fresh aim.

Our procedure, then, is to try (where necessary, with historical helps) to discern the function of a text in its own setting and then to see whether our attention is directed to considerations attending issues in our own situation which we might otherwise have ignored. That, of course, has always been a professed value in the study of ancient literature; but we begin with an additional, practiced assumption as well. Our working premise is that there is a certain identity or continuity between the "faith" which found superb expression in these separate writings and that which is confessed and is trying to express itself in ourselves. These historical texts are all valued elements of the Hebrew and Christian traditions. This makes it possible to ask what each text was up to by way of clarifying the nature and function of fundamental convictions, and to compare that with our own reflections. The goal is not to repeat, restate, or even apply these texts to situations they did not envision. It is, rather, to try to do in terms of our own concepts and engagements, what they did in terms of theirs.

It is often said that a chief problem confronting the Christian faith today is the problem of communication, that those who profess this faith may "know" it but don't know how to "say" it. Yet it is questionable whether we can really be said to know it until we have succeeded in expressing faith in terms of our own involvements and uninvolvements. There is a sense in which present issues and engagements are principles of textual interpretation, in which Christian understanding and proclamation arrive at the same time. Perhaps that is why Christian groups still not only study and teach but "preach" and "proclaim," and continue to ordain people to work at the latter task. This does not mean, of course, that the personnel, style, place, or manner of utterance must always remain the same. In a changing society, characterized by increasing specialization, we may expect that new expressions will be sought more cooperatively and nearer to points of common action than they have been in the past.

Though the truth they speak quells error's might, preachers are notoriously poor at remembering or acknowledging sources. We have preserved that dubious prerogative; accordingly, no notes are given with these chapters. Nevertheless, we might name certain specific helps which were especially influential or which might serve to clarify the particular point on which certain of the expositions hinge. Although the Book of Jonah contains only one eight-word prophetic oracle and is different in other ways from the prophetic writings, our understanding of its problem was facilitated by a number of current and choice books on the prophets. Here let us note merely that our interpretation does not follow more modern theodicy to speculation on the nature of God or on how his ways may be justified to man, but rather allows the book to present its own understanding of the nature and necessity of such questions—a necessity against which Jonah bumped his head but which is very unfamiliar to modern heads. This aspect of the question received a rare discursive treatment by G. Dennis O'Brien in an article entitled "Prolegomena to a Dissolution to the Problem of Suffering" appearing in *The Harvard Theological Review* for October, 1964.

A number of standard studies of the Gospel of Matthew help to place the story of the temptations in its structure and argument. We wish here to admit only what could never be denied: that these essays were conceived without once forgetting Dietrich Bonhoeffer's brief morning lectures entitled *Temptation*. Reflection on "the cup" in the sermon for Maundy Thursday was stimulated years ago by an article by C. U. Wolf, "Qumran and the Last Supper" (*Christian Century*, March 18, 1959), though his argument for a messianic cup at an original Last Supper is quite speculative. Israel's understanding of the kingship, on which the Good Friday sermon partly relies, is treated at length in Sigmund Mowinckel's chapter on the "royal psalms" in *The Psalms in Israel's Worship* (trans. D. R. Ap-Thomas [Nashville: Abingdon Press, 1962]) and in Helmer Ringgren's *The Messiah in the Old Testament* (Naperville, Ill.: Allenson, 1956), though many others have also treated this topic and everything debatable has been debated. Remarkable parallels between the kingship psalms and the passion narrative are unfolded in Barnabas Lindars' *New Testament Apologetic* (Philadelphia: Westminster Press, 1961). The treatment of the composition of John 20 in the Easter sermon was facilitated by the work of David Granskou, whose *Structure and Theology in the Fourth Gospel* is soon to be published. The interpretation of the language of that chapter reflects certain suggestions made by Ian Ramsey in *Religious Language* (New York: Macmillan Co., 1963). Finally, there are all the people with whom these texts have been shared in Princeton and Chicago and with whom passage was made "from faith to faith," in particular, Harold Remus there and Judith Reinken here, and Charles Whitman who helped prepare the manuscript.

Though these chapters are all somewhat longer than sermons dare to be (they reach out for additional biblical evidence in support of their interpretations and address several typical issues in each case), they nevertheless err on the side of deficiency. Two sorts of incompleteness should be noted from the outset since both set up continuing projects for the reader. The first has already been partially admitted. Many will find insufficient traditional dogmatic content in the exposition of these texts. Readers who are accustomed to making a distinction between "narrative" and "kerygma" in the biblical writings will note more use of the former than the latter. Our only explanation is that the kerygma is present in these narratives and vice versa, and that stories may have power to gain a fresh hearing where formulary proclamations have come to seem forbidding or dull. Others will miss repetitions of historic creedal formulations concerning the "person," "natures," and "work" of Jesus Christ. These are serious omissions, insofar as power may be lacking in tentative or partial affirmations. Yet the Christian faith today seems very much in the process of reappropriating Christ, with an eye both to past formulations and to newer criteria and issues. Every doctrine of Christ belongs to some city, and one does not deny the truth of the Christ of Chalcedon by saying we are still forming our talk about the Christ of Chicago. Better to clutch at that moving hem than to unfold preserved garments! There are many (some in the pews) who lose that crucial touch by hearing more than can be grasped or more than in any way grasps them. The seven weeks of Lent seem an auspicious period for beginning over in a simpler way with one who is a perpetual author and finisher of faith.

The other deficiency is just as serious and equally a matter for development. The current issues addressed in these essays are only sketched in outline; the details and colors need to be supplied. The emerging city is a focus for almost everyone today; the smallest hamlet is fundamentally affected by this vast new congeries of facts. One can spread an initial fan of issues confronting major groups in the society—black and poor, business and labor, professional and service people —and one can talk about the tasks of decision and reorganization in all these sectors. But it is impossible to predict which presently envisioned or unanticipated eventualities will have qualified those tasks before these essays come to print. In no case are the target and the language determined as they would be within any actual group of people confronting a concrete issue in terms of their own rhetoric and projects. In no case is the material shaped as it could be, and must be, in any actually functioning utterance. Let it be very clear that it is only in those further, fitted expressions that the word will join flesh to command action and summon song.

Here, then, are ten wooden blocks chopped down sufficiently to get them through the door. They still need to be trimmed and turned to single, penetrating points and then applied at precisely the right spots. The hilarity and solemnity which attend that practice are appropriate effects and provide the proper setting.

RICHARD HENRY LUECKE

Ash Wednesday, 1968
Urban Training Center
Chicago, Illinois

CONTENTS

Jonah and Nineveh:

Of Sleep and the City

ONE

None So
Soundly Sleep

*Now the word of the Lord came to Jonah the son of Amittai, say-
ing, "Arise, go to Nineveh, that great city, and cry against it; for
their wickeaness has come up before me." But Jonah rose to flee
to Tarshish from the presence of the Lord. He went down to Joppa
and found a ship going to Tarshish; so he paid the fare, and went
on board, to go with them to Tarshish, away from the presence
of the Lord.*

*But the Lord hurled a great wind upon the sea, and there was a
mighty tempest on the sea, so that the ship threatened to break up.
Then the mariners were afraid, and each cried to his god; and
they threw the wares that were in the ship into the sea, to lighten
it for them. But Jonah had gone down into the inner part of the
ship and lain down, and was fast asleep. So the captain came and
said to him, "What do you mean, you sleeper? Arise, call upon your
god! Perhaps the god will give a thought to us, that we do not
perish."*

*And they said to one another, "Come, let us cast lots, that we
may know on whose account this evil has come upon us." So they
cast lots, and the lot fell upon Jonah. Then they said to him, "Tell
us, on whose account this evil has come upon us? What is your
occupation? And whence do you come? What is your country?
And of what people are you?" And he said to them, "I am a
Hebrew; and I fear the Lord, the God of heaven, who made the
sea and the dry land." Then the men were exceedingly afraid, and
said to him, "What is this that you have done!" For the men knew
that he was fleeing from the presence of the Lord, because he had
told them.*

Then they said to him, "What shall we do to you, that the sea may quiet down for us?" For the sea grew more and more tempestuous. He said to them, "Take me up and throw me into the sea; then the sea will quiet down for you; for I know it is because of me that this great tempest has come upon you." Nevertheless the men rowed hard to bring the ship back to land, but they could not, for the sea grew more and more tempestuous against them. Therefore they cried to the Lord, "We beseech thee, O Lord, let us not perish for this man's life, and lay not on us innocent blood; for thou, O Lord, has done as it pleased thee." So they took up Jonah and threw him into the sea; and the sea ceased from its raging. Then the men feared the Lord exceedingly, and they offered a sacrifice to the Lord and made vows.

—Jonah 1:1–16

But Jonah had gone down into the inner part of the ship and had lain down, and was fast asleep.—Jonah 1:5

JONAH IS CALLED TO GO EAST over the desert to Nineveh, the reigning political and cultural center of his day. But we find him on a ship headed west with a one-way ticket to Tarshish, which was considered the end of the earth. Our first question is Why?

Why is this man running away? It would be easy enough for us to guess: anyone who has ever knocked on a strange door and hoped that nobody was home or who has ever felt strange about going alone to a big city or a foreign country (in Jonah's case it was to a city-nation which wore the boot). If we had to speak in that strange city to people who were unknown to us, who were in fact disposed to despise us, without any invitation or platform or honorarium, on a topic which (to say the least) was not likely to entertain or please them—well, we'd be reluctant too. It would be easy for us to take the story that way: Jonah is running away because he is simply and understandably scared.

But if we *do* understand Jonah's flight in that way we do so without a shred of evidence in the text, and in the face of every new stroke actually added by the writer. The story itself never suggests that Jonah is afraid of Nineveh or of any man in Nineveh. It is at pains to show that he is not even afraid of the sea, though he is a landlubber like every other Israelite. When all the other passengers are frantic with fear and crying in the storm, Jonah is in the hold of the ship, stretched out and fast asleep. That is not the behavior of a frightened man.

What the book actually says, in the second sentence, is that Jonah is running away "from the presence of the Lord." When, at the height of the storm, Jonah is asked to give an account of himself, what does he say? "I am a Hebrew; and I fear the Lord, the God of heaven, who made the sea and the dry land." That very belief somehow constitutes Jonah's problem, and the problem of the Book of Jonah. He fears the Lord above all things, above the sea and the dry land, above the storm, and above the city of Nineveh.

Why, then, is Jonah running away? Not primarily because he has a quarrel with Nineveh. His chief quarrel is with the Lord. He is not merely defying the elements; he is defying the Lord. His flight is not the result of unbelief; it is a result of his belief!

I

The Book of Jonah assumes that Jonah is a prophet with all that entailed in Israel. The first readers of this book remembered a prophet Jonah from the history of Israel. (The work of this eighth-century prophet is reported in II Kings.) A prophet was one who cared for the name of the Lord and demanded that this name should be kept holy by the people who had received it. Only in this way could it keep the people holy in a derived sense—which included keeping them separate from idols and "whole" in their response to one another and to new events.

A prophet was one who remembered the freedom of the Exodus from Egypt and the discipline of the wilderness. He repeated the promise and the command enfolded in those events, as these had been interpreted in Israel, for each new day. When the people entered the land of Canaan the prophets never allowed them to say, "This is it; the promise is now fulfilled." There were, by reference to both the Exodus and the conditions in the land, new ways to specify the demand and promise. When the people fell into the worship of the national gods of the Canaanites or into the practices of the folk religion which were supposed to make the grain grow and the cities thrive, the prophets pointed their attention to actual facts and issues in the name of the Lord. When the temple worship of the Lord became an instrument of idolatry, the currying of God's favor with special offerings while allowing complacency and injustice to flourish, it was the prophet (though occasionally an unofficial one) who stood outside the temple and said, "Take it home." When kings persisted in outworn alliances or uses of power which failed to meet the exigencies of justice in a new day, it was the prophet who repeated the story of the Exodus and said, "Now hear the word of the Lord." Prophets were among the few who contended for the Lord's name and the Lord's righteousness against the many in Israel who were ready to compromise it—and certainly against all who did not know it or who blasphemed it outside of Israel.

And now the prophet Jonah is supposed to go to Nineveh, the very city which the prophet Nahum described as "that well-formed whore," "the bloody city"? It wasn't just that Nineveh had everything—though it did. The public works of this capital of the Mesopotamian world were the marvel of its day, including an aqueduct which brought water thirty miles over the desert to parks and gardens, and a palace built on a shelf of twenty-five acres. Nineveh could boast the greatest library of its age, with polyglot dictionaries providing access to world literature. It had an efficient, no-nonsense army, as Israel came to know in its own turf and flesh. For a hundred years, Israel and Judah lived alternately beneath the heel of Nineveh or by its leave, always wondering when the Assyrian would come down like a wolf on the fold. When he finally did come down he put an end to Israel as a nation and played with Judah like a pawn for a hundred years more.

But for a prophet like Jonah, it was not merely that *Israel* seemed humiliated by a city like Nineveh—it was Israel's *Lord*. Assyrian pillars stood mocking, almost phallically, at many Israelite shrines, to be taken down and burned in one generation, only to stand there again in the next. On one occasion, Hezekiah paid tribute in the form of gold from the temple doors. Under Manasseh, Assyrian altars were built within the very precincts of the temple and prostitutes of both sexes were allowed to hustle a religious trade. A great "Aha!" hung in the air for years. Now, at a time when (as our text puts it) the wickedness of Nineveh had come up before the Lord, when its wickedness cried to heaven, when it seemed that the grapes of wrath were almost pressed and the cup was almost full for Nineveh—Jonah is called to go and *preach* there?

Jonah has a prophet's nose: he knows that the word of the Lord is not sent for naught. Later he as much as says that *this* had been his suspicion from the start and that *this* was why he had fled: "Is not this what I said when I was yet in my country? That is why I made haste to flee to Tarshish; for I knew that thou art a gracious God and merciful, slow to anger, and abounding in steadfast love, and repentest of evil" (4:2). The trouble was not that preaching to Nineveh was too "hard" for Jonah to do but that it was too "soft" for the Lord to do. It was not merely that the Lord seemed opposed to Jonah's wishes; it was that the Lord seemed to contradict his own will, that the Lord himself seemed wishy-washy. Many disaffected believers have complained against God that there is too much cruelty to the innocent in the world. Jonah complains that there is too much leniency to the guilty—and what hope is there for better things then? The statement of the question is different but the issue is the same, and Jonah's response is the same—conscientious objection!

If the Lord wanted to do with Nineveh what Jonah suspected he wanted to do with Nineveh, he could do it all right —but without Jonah. Was it for this that Israel had been led out of Egypt and disciplined for forty years in the wilderness? Was it for this that the prophets had contended? Did not an event so arbitrary rule out any further cooperation with God? Jonah was a preacher of righteousness; he was not one at this late date to start preaching a "cheap grace" or to start chirping about the "secular city."

It may be that we ourselves do not understand any of this, that we simply do not find ourselves responding any longer to what was bothering Jonah. Two results of what has been called the "death of God" (which may affect even those who still use his name) are that we no longer argue much with God and no longer run away from God. But let us be very clear that this also has something to do with how we look at the city, the emerging modern city no less than previous cities. Anyone can be critical about the modern city and anyone can be enthusiastic about it. There are many reasons for hating the modern city and many reasons for loving it, many reasons for running from the modern city and many reasons for returning to it. But what might it mean to acknowledge a "righteousness of God"—that is, a justice or a "rightness" which goes beyond what is specified in the laws and customs of the city—and *then* to learn slowness to anger and steadfast love? What would this mean for one's *participation* in the city, for both the manner and the extent of that participation? There are many ways to enter a city and many ways to see a city, but here would be a way of entering and seeing a city which is more than a matter of ordinary preference or predilection, of lust or disgust, a way described by one prophet as being "taught by God" (Isa. 54:13). That promise was picked up in the gospel: "And they shall all be taught by God" (John 6:45).

It is easy to love the city of one's dreams and easy to hate the bloody city, but how does one learn to *love* the *bloody* city? How does one learn to deal faithfully with the city that is? That is the kind of question which is raised by the Book of Jonah—even if it leaves us still squirming with that question at the end.

II

Let us return to the opening scene, to the sleep of Jonah, and ask our question again. Why does the prophet sleep? It would be easy enough, on the basis of behavior familiar to us, to understand this sleep as a means of escaping from heavy duties or from fear. It is common knowledge that people who are afraid of the future or uncertain of their abilities find it hard to get up in the morning and are inclined to take naps during the day. Insecure or bored housewives take sleeping pills or begin to tipple, unemployed men sleep through breakfast, and unsure businessmen numb themselves at lunch. Saul Bellow's Herzog observed that people are granted only two choices—to live or to die; but many of us keep looking for something in between.

If it is not fear which puts us to sleep, it may be favor. While he was Secretary of Health, Education, and Welfare, John W. Gardner warned the American public that it is difficult to "stay awake on a full stomach." The Marxists used to say that "false consciousness" arises from having property, especially when others have little, and that it takes an appropriate shock, like that of being separated from our property, to wake us up. It is an historical fact that new social stirrings are not readily seen by the comfortable. No fashionable commentator predicted anything approximating the French Revolution; few saw what was happening in Algeria; many simply shut their doors and drew their blinds during peaceful street demonstrations in American cities in earlier summers. It is easy for us to understand *that* kind of shut-eye, just as it is easy for us to understand *that* kind of flight from the city. But that, as we have seen, was not at all the case with Jonah, who was neither afraid nor uncertain, who saw what was going on in his world only too clearly, who cared about what he saw, and who responded to it in his own way.

We might be tempted, in terms of current cultural predilection, to interpret the sleep of Jonah as a picture of the "post-Christian" man. We are inclined these days to search the Scriptures for precedents of "secularity," and the prophets seem in certain respects to provide a happy hunting ground for this. On this view of the matter, Jonah's faith could be described as too mature to allow him to join with others in crying "each to his own god" to call off the storm. The only action that a really responsible man, a man come of age, could approve was throwing off the ballast. Even when that measure did not succeed Jonah did not lose his cool, and that, too, expresses something of the secular spirit. Remember how Albert Camus' "stranger" answered *his* interrogators and accepted his death in view of "the benign indifference of the universe?" No superstitions and no illusions intervened to soften or romanticize the blow. He fully expected life to come to a pointless end.

10

But that interpretation is also more than the text will bear (and it must be said that the text bears more than that interpretation). As for proscribing divine intervention in nature, the text itself cares little about that. The wind in the story is "hurled" by the Lord on the sea; the lot falls with deadly accuracy on Jonah; the fish, the plant, and the worm are all "appointed" by the Lord—these are commonplaces of this ancient story. Jonah does not hestitate for one moment to say that it was the Lord who sent the storm after him and that the same Lord would recall the storm after it had accomplished its purpose. That, moreover, is exactly what happens in the story. To be sure, the fear of death is not uppermost in Jonah's mind. But that is not to say it is a matter of *benign* indifference to him—nor (as we shall see) does he regard it as a matter of merely *benign* indifference in the universe.

Why, then, does Jonah sleep, if not because he is tired or afraid or indifferent? The answer must be that his is a deliberate sleep, a belligerent sleep. It is a posed indifference, a demonstration of non-participation. It is a sit-down or lie-down strike he is conducting against the very conditions of human existence. He is a dropout from the school of life. Like Job, who also had an "argument" with God, Jonah has seized on the one thing he can do to resist God: he can lie there, and if God smites him, he can die there—and thereby disappoint God! Jonah's sleep—even his death, if it comes to that—is aimed at God. Jonah does not sleep because he has lost his convictions. One might say he is sleeping to *save* his convictions, everything he has lived and worked for in the past. The sleep of Jonah is a rational, voluntary human act. If you believe in God but do not approve of his world there is nothing to *do* but to go your own way in it; and if you know you cannot really escape in that way then you can at least refuse to participate. If you believe in God but no longer wish to obey him, and if you know you really cannot flee him, there is nothing to *do* but sleep. None so soundly sleep as those who sleep the sleep of the believer.

11

Such an understanding is not peculiar to the Book of Jonah. The Book of Isaiah knows not only about a general listlessness in society, about "people who walked in darkness" or "dwelt in a land of deep darkness" (9:2); it also knows about a special blindness which may come to those who believe devoutly in God. "Who is blind but my servant, or deaf as my messenger whom I send? Who is blind as my dedicated one, or blind as the servant of the Lord?" (42:19). All Israelites sang a psalm which seems to be a poetic rendering of the story of Jonah:

> O that thou wouldst slay the wicked, O God,
>> and that men of blood would depart from me,
> men who maliciously defy thee,
>> who lift themselves up against thee for evil!
> Do not I hate them that hate thee, O Lord?
>> And do not I loathe them that rise up against thee?
> I hate them with perfect hatred,
>> I count them my enemies.

This psalm also knows that specific expectations based on assumptions about God are often overturned and that, when this happens, one tries—futilely—to run away:

> Whither shall I go from thy Spirit?
>> Or whither shall I flee from thy presence?
> If I ascend to heaven, thou art there!
> If I make my bed in Sheol, thou are there!
> If I take the wings of the morning
>> and dwell in the uttermost parts of the sea,
> even there thy hand shall lead me,
>> and thy right hand shall hold me.

The psalm closes with what must become the practical sum of the matter for faith—in which the "I's" become "me's" and God becomes the newly-trusted actor in every sentence:

> Search me, O God, and know my heart!
>> Try me and know my thoughts!
> And see if there be any wicked way in me,
>> and lead me in the way everlasting!   (Psalm 139)

III

To make this understanding of Jonah's sleep unmistakable, we are treated to a touching encounter between Jonah and the captain of the ship. What did Jonah mean, snoring away like that down there while the ship was on the verge of breaking up? Why didn't he at least *pray*? Fearful, half-believing souls often think fondly of prayer and like to be prayed for in times of difficulty. "It can't hurt." They wonder why believers don't pray more and why the church doesn't pray more, since we are beset by many and grave difficulties. Occasionally they wonder out loud.

But Jonah *knows* why he does not pray. The reason is not that he isn't sure whether prayer is answered or not; the reason is that he believes prayer *is* answered—unfortunately! The reason Christian people do not pray today (or pray only perfunctorily) may, of course, lie in the fact that they have become unbelieving or confused, that they are no longer sure whether there is any word from the Lord. But might not a further reason be that they suspect there *is* a word from the Lord and object to what might be required of them if it came? In particular, what they might have to do for that well-formed whore, the bloody city? Do we sleep so soundly partly because we *do* believe?

The church has long thought of itself as setting the agenda for the city or, in any case, for itself. What if issues in the city are now to help set the agenda for the church? For many years, the church has thought its primary task to be one of gathering people *in*. What if its primary task today is to turn its people *out* into the city? What if its people, some of whom have been content to pluck the city's fruits, must now agree to take up the city's problems, including those of distributing its fruits more equitably and even of enabling new pickers? For a long time the church has been engaged in works of charity. What if those works are now to be performed no worse, and possibly better, through public programs? What if the new call is to serve among the poor in new ways, ways

13

in which public programs cannot—helping them to raise their voices, claim their rights, exercise their power, and share in making the decisions and shaping the institutions which affect their lives? What if the new focus is to be not on the "church of God" in the city but on the "city of God" prayed for and served by the church? What if the Christian vision includes that of a *city* served by every member and so kept whole and in motion?

Might we not shrink from a preaching of repentance which could result in *that?* Might not all this seem so strange and so unfair to the church in view of its past struggles and triumphs—even so unfair to the church's Lord as it has previously known and taught him—that we would prefer to disobey the call, to run away, to let the storm come, to close our eyes and sleep the sleep of the believer?

IV

We wish at the close of each reflection on the Book of Jonah to turn to the New Testament, which speaks not only of the good man and strong believer Jonah but also of "something greater than Jonah" (Matt. 12:41; Luke 11:32).

Many of Jesus' activities, both his words and deeds, may be seen as attempts to wake people up—first of all, believing people. His basic proclamation, according to the Gospels, was "Repent, for the kingdom of heaven is at hand" (Matt. 4:17; Mark 1:14). This proclamation meant in effect: Wake up to the new thing happening before your eyes; live now in the light of the future which God will bring. In parable after parable, episode after episode, someone did or did not respond to the alarm clock, someone either came to new light or remained in darkness, someone either woke to new joy or walked away sorrowfully—in the latter case, as often as not, condemned out of his own snoring mouth.

When it came to the hour of his passion, what did Jesus say to his disciples except that they should stay awake? "Watch with me and pray!" But while he watched and prayed, they

14

slept. They were not merely sleeping out of weariness—Luke says they were "sleeping for sorrow." This was not what they had expected, either for themselves or for their Lord. This was why they alternately drew their swords and ran away. It was this sleep of the disciples, of those who might have been expected to be most awake, which called forth the rich irony of the Gospels: "Sleep on now and take your rest. . . ."

A New Testament epistle distinguishes between people who are "children of light" and people who are "children of darkness," and sings a promise to anyone who is willing to open his eyes: "Awake, O sleeper, and arise from the dead, and Christ shall give you light" (Eph. 5:14). It speaks of "making the most of the time," even in dark days, as a result of waking to that light. Another epistle speaks directly to "sons of the day," telling them to *stay* awake: "So then let us not sleep, as others do, but let us keep awake and be sober." That seems to be the trick: to stay awake *and* sober. It is easy enough to be awake in the modern city if you are not sober, or to be sober if you are not awake. But to be *both*—that is the demand and the promise of faith. That could lead to the discovery of new possibilities and actions for the city.

At the close of *A Sleep of Prisoners,* Christopher Fry laments the fact that people have always been reluctant to wake up, though seldom more dangerously so than they are today:

It takes
So many thousand years to wake.
But will you wake for pity's sake?
Wake up, will you!

In a poem called "Walking to Sleep," Richard Wilbur speaks of how the will to sleep can become resolute and unturning.

What you hope for
Is that at some point of the pointless journey,
Indoors or out, and when you least expect it,
Right in the middle of your stride, like that,

15

So neatly that you never feel a thing,
The kind assassin Sleep will draw a bead
And blow your brains out.

What is bothering Christopher Fry is what might happen if we
don't wake up. What is bothering Richard Wilbur, and what
he says is bothering us, is what might have to happen if we do!

TWO

Awake in the Deep

The 2nd lesson is written in the 1st chapter of Jonah - beginning with 17th verse,

And the Lord appointed a great fish to swallow up Jonah; and Jonah was in the belly of the fish three days and three nights.

Then Jonah prayed to the Lord his God from the belly of the fish, saying,

> "I called to the Lord, out of my distress,
>   and he answered me;
> out of the belly of Sheol I cried,
>   and thou didst hear my voice.
> For thou didst cast me into the deep,
>   into the heart of the seas,
>   and the flood was round about me;
> all thy waves and thy billows
>   passed over me.
> Then I said, 'I am cast out
>   from thy presence;
> how shall I again look
>   upon thy holy temple?'
> The waters closed in over me,
>   the deep was round about me;
> weeds were wrapped about my head
>   at the roots of the mountains.
> I went down to the land
>   whose bars closed upon me for ever;
> yet thou didst bring up my life from the Pit,
>   O Lord my God.
> When my soul fainted within me,
>   I remembered the Lord;
> and my prayer came to thee,
>   into thy holy temple.

17

Those who pay regard to vain idols
  forsake their true loyalty.
But I with the voice of thanksgiving
  will sacrifice to thee;
 what I have vowed I will pay.
  Deliverance belongs to the Lord!"

And the Lord spoke to the fish, and it vomited out Jonah upon the dry land.

—Jonah 1:17–2:10

Here endeth the Lesson,

Deliverance belongs to the Lord!—Jonah 2:9

IN THE FIRST CHAPTER OF JONAH
we learned to distinguish a very special kind of sleep: the
sleep of the believer. This sort of sleep is not simply a result
of having heavy or drooping eyes; it is a result of deliberately closing one's eyes. It is not a matter of not seeing or of not
being able to see what is going on but a matter of *having* seen,
of not liking what one has seen, and of not wanting to look
anymore. It is not merely a matter of having seen certain un-
pleasant facts of life and being wary of new facts; for one who
sleeps in this way the facts of life are not worth knowing.
Jonah was immobilized as a matter of belief but not because of
any too-simple belief that God would intervene to save him.
That kind of belief was more characteristic of the other men on
the ship. Jonah was paralyzed because he was having, or was
trying to have, a strangely complicated argument with
God.

We are often full of good advice for people who turn their
faces away from life and we are not disinclined to give that advice, especially if their attitude becomes annoying to us, if they
get to be a drag, as we say. What people like that need, we
volunteer, is to come to their senses: they need to see that
such attitudes are getting them nowhere, that they are really
hurting no one but themselves, or that it wouldn't be so bad
if they were only hurting themselves but they are also hurting
other people. What such people need to do, we say, is to pull
themselves together, pluck up and make some fresh resolution.
If they don't like things the way they are they should take
steps to change them. If they find that difficult, perhaps they
have a vitamin deficiency and should try a new diet or drug.
Maybe what they need is a good rest or a change of scenery: a
few weeks in the country or a cruise, a new romantic interest
or a night on the town.

If they simply cannot pull themselves out of the bog in any of these ways, we are inclined to suggest a visit to a good psychiatrist, who might help them uncover unacknowledged reasons for their feelings of depression. If they insist that their feelings are not pathological but valid, they might at least find some creative expression for them. They might write a poem, or put a favorite record on the stereo. They could see a play: if musical comedy seems too bubbly for their tastes, they might choose a tragedy about someone who is even worse off than they are or about someone who is better off than they are but who comes to a worse end. Best of all, they might see a tragi-comedy, which shows that nothing is so tragic but that it is also comic, and vice versa.

All these measures have a certain validity. Despondent spirits often respond surprisingly to such treatments. But we have seen why none of these tactics is really appropriate to the kind of complaint described in the first chapter of Jonah. Jonah's problem was not primarily one of emotions or "nerves"; it was intellectual and moral—or, to be precise, theological. Jonah did not need to "come to his senses"; he saw things clearly enough—too clearly, it seemed to him. He did not need to be told where his attitude might lead, or that he was hurting only himself, for he fully accepted the possibility that this was the end for him. There was no use in telling him to do something about it; his attitude required his taking no action at all. He knew there were brighter scenes elsewhere but he wasn't going to let himself be cajoled by them. His cruise and his sleep were not for the purpose of changing his point of view; they were rather the consequences of his point of view. He needed no psychiatrist to uncover the source of his despair for he knew the cause. Diagnosis was not needed and diversion was not appropriate. To avoid such temptations he had taken his boots off and gone to sleep.

As a last stratagem Jonah might have given his attitude doleful or heroic expression in poetry (no one who writes or sings is entirely devoid of enthusiasm). In the second chapter, in fact, Jonah does turn to poetry. But the poem is not a

20

lament, or a blues, or a song of defiance. Jonah is not, in this song, an exemplary hero or soulful poet expressing himself in the face of an implacable and unfeeling nature. Nor is he simply whistling in the dark to pluck up his spirits. The song does not focus on the poet himself or on his feelings—it is a "song of deliverance." It is a song which celebrates the one thing which can awaken a man from the sleep of the believer. And singing this song is the first thing a man so awakened will do.

I

Many of us will find a familiar cadence, as well as some familiar images, in the song of Jonah. We have heard words like these before and have even spoken and sung similar words together. "Out of the depths I cry to thee, O Lord," "All thy waves and thy billows have gone over me," "For my soul is full of troubles and my life draws near to Sheol"—these are well-known expressions from the Hebrew psalms. The song of Jonah is not meant to be read as a spontaneous composition down there among the juices, any more than Aeneas should be thought to have spoken in iambic pentameter in every desperate strait. Rather, its readers were to hear in the song of Jonah the very kind of song which they all sang, and see its images as depicting fundamental characteristics of faith in any time or place.

Students of Hebrew poetry classify the song of Jonah with a particular type of biblical psalm. The singer or speaker in this group of psalms appears to be standing in the temple, telling the people that he had fallen into some great extremity, that he had then called on God and was delivered, and that he wished now to make a sacrifice of thanksgiving in the great congregation. But the testimonial has assumed a polished, poetic form, which everyone can join in singing. The song of Jonah is not simply a private utterance out of a particular experience in the ocean; it is the kind of song used by everyone in the temple, even by people who never went down to the sea. It

21

is a paradigmatic song of faith, which can be sung (and, in a sense, must be sung) by every faithful man.

All these familiar, poetic words about the water—about being cast "into the deep, into the heart of the seas," about the surrounding "flood" and the engulfing "waves" and "billows"—refer, to be sure, to the watery floundering of Jonah when he was cast overboard, but they also denote a "death" which attends us all and toward which we all sometimes sink. In the psalms, water often symbolized death, perhaps because in ancient cosmology the earth was thought to have emerged from (and to be continually threatened by) the primeval chaos of water, or because of the recurring cycle in nature of the water in the clouds coming to earth and then returning to the clouds through evaporation, or because when water is poured out on the ground it is irretrievable. The song of Jonah combined this water-image of death with a widely-shared image of the earth to produce a most memorable picture. The earth itself was thought to protrude out of the waters, and to be held up by the mountains which had their base at the bottom of the sea. Accordingly, the place or abode of death was pictured at the very lowest point of the physical world, below the earth, in the waters at the base of the mountains. Now do we understand this picture?

> The waters closed in over me,
>   the deep was round about me;
> weeds were wrapped about my head
>   at the roots of the mountains.
> I went down to the land
>   whose bars closed on me for ever.

To fully appreciate this song, we will have to consider death as something one "sinks toward." It is not merely a terminal fact but a direction or movement of diminishing vitality, toward a point where, wrapped about by weeds, there is no longer any hope of reversing one's direction. The Hebrew could speak of "dying" as taking place even while a man was in no immediate danger of ending his days. Any weakness or

22

dissolution of powers amounted to "dying"; any new strength or new coordination of powers amounted to "living." Samson would break out of his ropes, fight a thousand Philistines, and become dead-tired; but when he drank from the gushing rock, "his spirit returned, and he lived" (Judg. 15:19). When the Hebrews shouted, "Let the King live!" they meant that he should enjoy prosperity, victory, influence, and wisdom, as well as a long reign. The promise that children who respected their parents would "live long on the earth" referred not merely to length of days but to healthy and harmonious days as well.

Something of this sinking toward death in the midst of life is echoed in our own phrases. We sink into our chairs and say "I'm dead" or "I feel half-dead." In the face of some crucial eventuality, we say, "If that happens I'm dead," even though we expect to go on living and breathing. Occasionally we even say, as Jonah did, that we've "been through hell." When we think of death, we regret not only that our life will come to an end but that we haven't been very much alive along the way. On a billboard message, "Millions now living will never die," a wag once changed the last three words to read: "Millions now living were never alive." Sometimes it is asked in big-city elections (or in large congregations) whether all the people on the list are still alive; and one is often tempted to reply, "Yes, but there are lots of borderline cases!"

Even after what we customarily call death has taken place, the Hebrews thought of a man as existing in a distended, weakened, disunited form—in bones, name, descendants, works, and property. "Sheol" was a popular word for that condition, in which all that remains of a man is breathless, juiceless, unthinking, scattered, and inert beyond recovery. The Book of Ezekiel envisions the elite of many nations dry and motionless in Sheol. Israel itself is seen as a valley of "dry bones," and the question is asked, "Can these bones live?" (Ezek. 37:3). Certainly not by their taking any thought or resolution, or by any agency of their own! Just that, surely, is what Jonah wishes to assert from the very outset of his song: "Out of the belly of Sheol I cried." He cries not out of "no

23

existence" but out of his utter helplessness to move again in the direction of life. What he is up against is not the kind of problem which he can solve by ordinary action. For physical ailments one can take medicines; for emotional disturbances one can seek therapy; for tragic insights one can write poems —but none of these measures speaks to Jonah's question. They all amount to placebos which only do violence to his question. Therefore Jonah describes his condition—one which can very well occur at the height of one's physical, intellectual, emotional, and artistic powers—in terms of life's lowest and most helpless state. We sometimes speak about death as a "sleep"; Jonah here speaks about his "sleep" as a "death."

This passivity of Jonah's condition and the "outside" source of what it took to wake him up are made unmistakable by the very form of the Hebrew psalm, by the alternations between "I" and "thou" in verse after verse.

> Out of the belly of Sheol *I* cried,
>   and *thou* didst hear my voice. . . .
> *I* went down to the land
>   whose bars closed upon me for ever;
> yet *thou* didst bring up my life from the Pit,
>   O Lord my God.

Deliverance, if it was to come at all, had to come from the Lord.

But before Jonah arrives at that he comes to see something else. He comes to see the "death" which he has been talking about as something more than *his* way of fleeing from, or *his* way of protesting against, the Lord. He comes to see his own last weapon as not outside the purview of the Lord. Death was not only Jonah's defiant messenger to the Lord; it was, at the same time, the Lord's loyal messenger to him.

II

While he was on board ship, Jonah had been strangely silent. He had not expressed his thoughts or followed them

24

through to their conclusions; he had not tried to help save the ship nor had he raised a hand against himself. He simply slept. Now, when he opens his mouth to speak from the sea it is to admit something which has been true from the start, even though it has heretofore gone unexpressed: the very isolation and immobility which he had found in his flight, even the death which presently threatened, were from the Lord. "For *thou* didst cast me into the deep . . . all *thy* waves and *thy* billows passed over me." Seen in its brute objectivity, death did not merely represent a way *out* of the demands made upon Jonah; it also represented those very demands *to* him. Though he had asked to be thrown into the sea, it was not *his* waves and *his* billows that bore in on every side.

The prophets often referred to death in preaching judgment. They did so not primarily because people were afraid of death and could be manipulated in this way, but because "death" afforded a way of pointing to demands more encompassing than those imposed by the special projects people chose for themselves. One must go out of his intended way to stave off death; and death puts an end to the best-laid plans of men. For Jonah to imagine that he could exempt himself from new, uncongenial duties because he had no precedent for them was to give up the very thing for which he had always contended. It was to commit the simplistic fallacy of limiting God, to fall into the very idolatry which he condemned in a competent but feckless Nineveh. If he persisted in such an attitude he would become the object of his own bitter rumbling. He'd be hoist by his own petard!

Jonah's God was a jealous God: He could not be altogether subjected to rules or purposes which customarily guide behavior. A king or a general may offer, as the reason for obeying him, "Because I'm the king," "Because I'm in command." A lover sometimes refuses to ask what the reasons are for his love. To offer considerations for obeying, or for loving, makes the relationship—which the king and the lover wish to assert as beyond question—open to question. Of course, reasons *can* be given for political and military authority, and there are reasons why lovers should or should not consider marriage, reasons which leave both kings and suitors subject to question and review. But it is important to see the sense in which this would not be the case with Jonah's Lord: for we are really dealing with the Lord only if there is no asking the question whether he deserves to be obeyed or whether he loves. Jonah is arguing with one who could use the very futility of that protest to bring Jonah to a fresh perception.

Since Jonah's God is a jealous God he may be expected to assert his will or his love in a jealous way. Kings and lovers have been known to issue arbitrary demands simply to test obedience or devotion to themselves. The greatest sufferer is likely to be one who has been most loyal but who now finds himself overruled, seemingly arbitrarily, for new favorites. Similarly, in the Scriptures, when someone devoted to God begins to think he can predict continued favors for himself, or imminent downfall for others, he is likely to find himself thrown to a fish or scraping boils or otherwise afflicted with a lesson in faith. The purpose of such stories is not simply to describe a relationship of power to powerlessness. (For neither are we to worship prefabricated concepts like "all-powerfulness" or even "all-goodness," either of which might result in something obnoxious.) The point of such stories is that we are to *watch* for new opportunities and demands disclosed within the world, confident that "those who wait on the Lord will never be confounded," even when their previous expectations are (wholesomely) denied.

III

Jonah's returning awareness may be something for which we ourselves have little taste or patience. For us, death has for the most part lost that earlier significance. It has become less an occasion of contemplation and more a cause of technical projects. Astonishing victories have been won precisely by viewing death as a natural, objective phenomenon to be studied and managed like all other phenomena. Unprecedented new possibilities have been brought into view: not only the defeat of disease and famine but the replacement of defective limbs and organs by mechanical devices, glandular rejuvenation for the infirmities of old age, and even "freezing" bodies for resuscitation in some future age. We usually speak of death as the point at which nothing more is to be done for a man's organic life. Hair and cuticles may continue to grow in the grave, but the man is "dead" specifically when his heart has stopped beyond resuscitation (though that definition is in the process of being extended through heart transplants and is being debated by those who wish on occasion to substitute brain damage as a criterion). We also speak of "life" as a scientific project. We speak of "synthesizing life" by constructing self-replicating molecules, and it has come within the range of possibility to synthesize chosen combinations of "inherited" characteristics. We are pleased and excited to be engaged in this kind of project and we do not wish the new demands for technical competence to be compromised in any way by superstition or fear.

With all this (though he would have understood very little of it), Jonah's new faith would not need to quarrel. On the contrary, investigations might be conducted most freely by men who do not ask beforehand whether the results will be worth knowing and who are disposed to be trustful of whatever is discovered. The question is whether we are able to learn from Jonah something less familiar to us. Are we able to see demands revealed to us and imposed upon us which are not simply identical with the problems we have chosen to take up? Demands which require our accepting additional problems, or our taking up problems we might otherwise have preferred to ignore? Demands, for example, that we not only increase the number of our goods and services but also arrange for more equitable distribution of needed goods in our own cities and in the nations of the world? Demands that we not only offer our services to the needy but also make room for them to offer theirs? Do we see the need to take up problems not required by law or by previous societal expectations? Is it clear that public measures in housing, education, job training, and motivational training will succeed only partially unless they can be used to develop economic and political power within communities of the poor? If the rich are reluctant to respond to such gestures by the poor, do we see the need to address the problem that reluctance presents—to contend with attitudes of fatness? Do we see this as included in our understanding of the demands made upon us as men in our situation? Do we see how life itself imposes such demands, even though they are never fully set down in writing or universally accepted?

Might we not even see degrees of "death" or "dying," to use Jonah's term, in any refusals to respond to such demands —even at times when we are still, in our own terms, alive and kicking? Might not we who speak of "the death of God" because we do not want to give up human responsibility for human problems, learn with Jonah to think also of "the God of death"—who does not solve our problems for us but compels us to become problem-solvers, and who uses physical, social, and political threats to summon us to take up more and more problems? Both sides of this—Jonah's use of death to flee the Lord and the Lord's use of death to reclaim Jonah, our use of "the death of God" to assert our own manhood and a further understanding of that "death" as calling us to fully responsive manhood—have found expression in a new litany for Good Friday:

℣: God is dead.

℟: Thanks be to God!

IV

If we compare the story of Jonah with New Testament accounts of Jesus, we find ourselves comparing two men, neither of whom ran away from death (which may be *our* characteristic response to the prospect of death). We find in Jonah a man who thought he could flee *into* death, thereby escaping life's demands, until he saw death not only as an escape but also as

28

a sign of those demands. "If I make my bed in Sheol, thou art there!" In Jesus we find a man who saw this and something more, who learned obedience, or the very way of life, in facing his death. In the struggle of Gethsemane, Jesus prayed to a Father who did not intervene to take away the impending ordeal, not even for a beloved or innocent son. What Jesus saw in prayerfully confronting his own death was a will which went beyond what one might otherwise choose for himself or wish for others. "My Father, if it be possible, let this cup pass from me; nevertheless, not as I will, but as thou wilt" (Matt. 26:39). This watchful contention reached the critical point when Jesus cried from the cross the words of a Hebrew psalm: "My God, my God, why hast thou forsaken me?" God did not step in to loose the nails, strike down the detractors, and give public awards to those who trusted him. He allowed men to debate him, deny him, run from him, even crucify his faithful son. Yet precisely in this way, when the running and the shouting had ceased, a new form of response was born which brought an unexpected, incomparable gift of its own. To know more fully what it is to respond as a man in the world—to see oneself as called to share in a future larger than the one he previously envisioned, to know oneself as judged in his failure and upheld in the possibility so to respond—that made the night as bright as the day and gave a song in the deep.

All that the death of Jesus holds for the Gospels was not included in Jonah's song about death. But a crucial point has been reached and passed when Jonah no longer merely runs or sleeps but begins to listen again. In that moment, Jonah's thought of death no longer enfolds a despair of life; it now includes a previously resisted idea that life has not yet despaired of him. He has reached the nadir of his flight and has turned around, or has *been* turned around. To be sure, he still has something to learn (in particular, how to view the bloody city). But as Simon Peter began to look to Christ from the waves, Jonah has turned from death toward life. He has gotten the seaweed out of his ears. He is moving in the right direction again—and that in itself is worth a song!

A modern composer, whose work is not often heard, writes long intervals of "silence" into his music and has even written a book by that title. He wishes to call attention to voices in our environment which go unheeded until we become attuned to them. There is today, if we may borrow his theme, a vast environmental roar of technological and social change, as yet largely inaudible because we have not devised conceptions and institutions to take account of it and because we continue to fill the air with noises to which we are accustomed. The change is no less real because of that; its waves are washing around our ears, whispering, murmuring, shouting unprecedented opportunities and new demands. Could it be that if we started to listen again we too would find reason to wake up—and even to sing?

THREE

Learning to Love the Bloody City

Then the word of the Lord came to Jonah the second time, saying, "Arise, go to Nineveh, that great city, and proclaim to it the message that I tell you." So Jonah arose and went to Nineveh, according to the word of the Lord. Now Nineveh was an exceedingly great city, three days' journey in breadth. Jonah began to go into the city, going a day's journey. And he cried, "Yet forty days, and Nineveh shall be overthrown!" And the people of Nineveh believed God; they proclaimed a fast, and put on sackcloth, from the greatest of them to the least of them.

Then tidings reached the king of Nineveh, and he arose from his throne, removed his robe, and covered himself with sackcloth, and sat in ashes. And he made proclamation and published through Nineveh, "By the decree of the king and his nobles: Let neither man nor beast, herd nor flock, taste anything; let them not feed, or drink water, but let man and beast be covered with sackcloth, and let them cry mightily to God; yea, let everyone turn from his evil way and from the violence which is in his hands. Who knows, God may yet repent and turn from his fierce anger, so that we perish not?"

When God saw what they did, how they turned from their evil way, God repented of the evil which he had said he would do to them; and he did not do it.

But it displeased Jonah exceedingly, and he was angry. And he prayed to the Lord and said, "I pray thee, Lord, is not this what I said when I was yet in my country? That is why I made haste to flee to Tarshish; for I knew that thou art a gracious God and merciful, slow to anger, and abounding in steadfast love, and repentest of evil. Therefore now, O Lord, take my life from me, I beseech thee, for it is better for me to die than to live." And the Lord said, "Do you do well to be angry?" Then Jonah went out of the city and sat to the east of the city, and made a booth for himself there. He sat under it in the shade, till he should see what would become of the city.

And the Lord God appointed a plant, and made it come up over Jonah, that it might be a shade over his head, to save him from his discomfort. So Jonah was exceedingly glad because of the plant. But when dawn came up the next day, God appointed a worm which attacked the plant, so that it withered. When the sun rose, God appointed a sultry east wind, and the sun beat upon the head of Jonah so that he was faint; and he asked that he might die, and said, "It is better for me to die than to live." But God said to Jonah, "Do you do well to be angry for the plant?" And he said, "I do well to be angry, angry enough to die." And the Lord said, "You pity the plant, for which you did not labor, nor did you make it grow, which came into being in a night, and perished in a night. And should not I pity Nineveh, that great city, in which there are more than a hundred and twenty thousand persons who do not know their right hand from their left, and also much cattle?"

—Jonah 3–4

But God said to Jonah, "Do you do well to be angry for the plant?" And he said, "I do well to be angry, angry enough to die." And the Lord said, "You pity the plant, for which you did not labor, nor did you make it grow, which came into being in a night and perished in a night. And should not I pity Nineveh, that great city, in which there are more than a hundred and twenty thousand persons who do not know their right hand from their left, and also much cattle?"—Jonah 4:9–11

I

AT LAST WE FIND JONAH where he was to have gone from the start—at Nineveh, the city on the make. The question is whether he can take what he has learned—the hard way—back to that city. Coming to terms with oneself and coming to terms with the city may seem two different things (though they have much to do with each other) and Jonah is having his difficulties with the latter. We find him doing some very strange things: first kicking the ground inside the city, and then building a little cabin for himself outside the city limits.

Once again our question is Why? What exactly is bothering the prophet? And once more we must be very careful because we are always tempted to read a story like this in terms of our own predilections or previous assumptions. In that case, we will not learn anything from the story which we were not prepared to accept at the outset; we will not gain anything from the text which we did not bring to it.

It would be easy enough, in terms of a certain set of notions we might bring to this text, to come to an altogether current and choice interpretation of Jonah's cabana in the sun. There he sits outside the city limits in his little house, "till he should see what would become of the city." Now, that is a familiar picture. Think of all the people who flee the city limits, build a little house, and then sit in it, leaving the city to work out its own problems. Think of all the people who are simply "spectators" of the modern city, who sit and wonder whether

33

the city will ever become a viable and humane place for all its citizens to live in, who speculate whether the marches and civil contention are helping the city or setting it back, or who are waiting to see what time will tell (forgetting that what time will tell may well depend on what people like themselves do in the meantime).

We could say that this is what Jonah was doing—washing his hands of the whole affair, or at least keeping them clean. He had no roots in that city; besides, the city was no place for a religious man. It was, after all, a wicked and violent place. Even the king knew what knavery was going on in the city, for his proclamation admitted as much. "Let everyone turn from his evil way and from the violence which is in his hands."

The very opportunities of the city make it fertile soil for "evil ways." The city is a place to get rich, and for some people that is all it is. The city is a place where you can do things which can't be done so freely in a small town. So, for some, the city is a place where one can get rich by selling things which cannot be bought and sold so freely in a small town. The wealth accruing from such enterprises has sometimes been sufficient to force an informal alliance with the powers that be, or with the powers that want to be. Simply getting things done in the city—at least as long as people in the suburbs withhold their support from city interests in the state legislature—often requires a strong party organization, a judicious distribution of patronage and contracts, and a network of informal relationships which the opposition is quick to call "the machine." "City politics" is a phrase many find hard to use without a slur. It all seems very corrupt and also quite necessary.

As for "violence," the very conglomerate makeup of big cities is conducive to strife and explosive disorder. This is even more the case during times of rapid migration to the city when there are insufficient provisions for receiving and "civilizing" all who come. A new Negro tenant in a white neighborhood, a group of civil rights marchers, a word or jostle in a crowd which might have racial overtones, a hasty judgment by a policeman with no knowledge of Spanish, any of these is enough to touch off a rumble or a rebellion. Germans have marched against Irish, Italians against Poles, white housewives against black school children, and blacks have turned against white business establishments in their own neighborhoods. Meanwhile, the Minutemen, citizens' councils, and Hell's Angels announce their readiness to ride out as private avengers. Cries of "police brutality" on one side are met by calls for "law and order" on the other. Almost every night while watching Huntley-Brinkley, we shake our heads over violence in one city or another—between commercials, before going to supper.

That's it: Jonah is sitting in front of his television set. He had been willing enough to conduct a mission to the city but now he has withdrawn to a safer place. This is a text for the "suburban church" or the "suburban man"!

But this interpretation really won't do. Partly because the modern stereotype we have sketched simply cannot be made to fit Jonah: there was no element of exploitation in Jonah, no fleeing the city's problems while plucking the city's fruits. And partly because of what he says explicitly. Jonah is no indifferent spectator. He cares passionately about what happens to the city, he is personally involved in how it all comes out, and he is willing to stake his life on the outcome. If it doesn't come out the way he thinks it should, he doesn't want to live anymore. If the city is not destroyed, then *he* is willing to be destroyed.

We might (trying again) focus on this very desperation in Jonah to find another modern picture. An article in *The Village Voice* commemorating the sixth anniversary of SNCC and describing a growing desperation among American black people was entitled "Two Cheers for the Death Wish." A city which has repeatedly ignored, frustrated, and betrayed the peaceful demands of a particular group of people for equal opportunities, and which continues to do so even after the facts have been exposed, may seem to have lost its legitimacy and to deserve destruction. When every attempt at reform fails, say the oppressed, rebellion must come—and if that rebellion is simply crushed by greater power, they are willing to be destroyed with it. If the city will not let a man be human in a rational, political way, he may deem it essential to be human in a more radical, supra-political way—even if he fails.

Is this what Jonah is saying? He is, after all, a member of a minority. His people were at various times subjected to economic exploitation, political humiliation, forced deportation, and "police brutality" at the hands of Nineveh. For many decades Israel lived alternately beneath Nineveh's swinging stick or by its "protection." Nineveh was not called the "bloody city" for nothing: was not Samaria put to the sword by Nineveh and Jerusalem held helpless beneath its blade? Are Jonah's words then the voice of a suffering minority which longs to cry "Burn, baby, burn"?

There is some plausibility and perhaps a certain validity in that. But even this does not fully encompass the prophet's complaint, which is directed primarily not against Nineveh but against the Lord. Here in the last chapter we finally hear Jonah's own desperation at what has been nagging him from the start: "Is not this what I said when I was yet in my country? That is why I made haste to flee to Tarshish; for I knew that thou art a gracious God and merciful, slow to anger, and abounding in steadfast love, and repentest of evil. Therefore, now, O Lord, take my life from me, I beseech thee, for it is better for me to die than to live." A question arises: Does he "do well to be angry"? But Jonah has no ears for any such question as yet.

Nineveh was no novice in the ways of wickedness and violence, but it was in Jonah's eyes a complete novice in the ways of the Lord and his righteousness. Now, when the cup of wickedness was full in Nineveh, when the time had come for those who had taken up the sword to taste the sword—thereby showing the righteousness of the Lord in the earth—should the city be allowed to repent and judgment to pass over?

It is not hard to extrapolate reflections which give substance to Jonah's complaint. What could that repentance really amount to—a fast promptly instituted by a people who feared destruction, sackcloth and ashes put on by an astute king? Popular religion is notoriously shallow and superstitious, especially when it seeks to preserve prosperity and avert disaster. Religious utterances by public officials are always likely to be opportunistic and condescending. There was something far too easy about saying at this late hour, "Let everyone turn from his evil way and from the violence which is in his hands." Such mile-wide religiosity could hardly be more than an inch deep. It called forth no deep thoughts about the world or about the Lord. That such shallowness should now be rewarded was the last straw.

On the other side of such reflections lay even plainer facts. Defeat and humiliation did *not* always pass over Israel. Jonah was not naive about Israel itself, imagining that it deserved nothing but prosperity from the Lord. He knew about the "chastening" of this "firstborn son"; as a prophet he might have used such terms in interpreting the sufferings in Israel. But if judgment and destruction were *always* to befall the people who bore the Lord's name, while turning aside again and again from the people who blasphemed that name, what could anybody learn from *that?* If nothing could *ever* be depended upon to happen on the basis of one's faith, was not faith thereby rendered simply meaningless? If the Lord was simply capricious, wasn't that like having no Lord at all? Wasn't it the Lord himself who was cheapening the Lord's name? Wouldn't it be right to withhold one's worship from such a God? Even to resign from his world?

To Jonah it seemed that the time had come to have this out. He wanted a showdown then and there. This was for Jonah what a modern might call a "paradigm case," a case that decided the matter. Therefore he stages his vigil: he goes outside the city limits, builds himself a booth, and sits there in that box seat, arms folded over his chest, to see what will happen—or not happen—next. The Lord would have to consider both the city *and* this determined witness against the city. It is as though Jonah is saying, "All right, go ahead with it or don't go ahead with it—but remember, I'm watching!"

II

Now for the treatment, which in the biblical stories is always hardest on those who believe or are most beloved. In this case the treatment is administered by means of a plant and a question. A plant grows up over Jonah's booth, providing a few hours of relief from the desert heat. Jonah is surprised and delighted. The next morning when the sun returns, a worm attacks the plant and it withers to the ground. Nothing is more "burned" than Jonah who feels newly toyed-with by the Lord's plant and the Lord's worm, and repeats his former complaint about wishing to die. This time the question put to Jonah is specifically about the plant: "Do you do well to be angry for the plant?" Jonah's reply is as testy and unhesitating as ever: Yes, he has every right to be angry—"angry enough to die."

This answer is very interesting if we think about it. Jonah is made to think about it in two steps: by a descriptive sentence and a concluding question—first the indicative, then the interrogative. "You pity the plant, for which you did not labor, nor did you make it grow, which came into being in a night, and perished in a night." Was Jonah forgetting the sheer actuality of things even before he did anything about them— was he forgetting the waves and the billows? The plant came as a sheer gift, as in the last analysis (or *before* any analysis) all things do. There was, with respect to this plant, no legal or contractual claim at all, no appeal to justice or to what was his due. Yet Jonah *was* making demands concerning that plant. Wasn't there a certain incongruity in that, enough to give a moment's pause? Wasn't there a secret enfolded in Jonah's surprise and delight over the fortuitous plant which was not irrelevant for any joy whatever? Doesn't the interposition of one's own expectations and demands destroy the very point of any delight? When, for example, a little boy eats an ice-cream cone and cries at the same time because there might not be another! Or when a woman frowns and complains to her husband while she is bending over a strawberry parfait! While we're still on the subject, wasn't there something strangely incongruous about Jonah's enjoying himself in the shade, or his lamenting the loss of that shade to himself, and at the same time wishing himself *dead?*

The point can now be made. As Jonah was not in any position to make any final demands about the plant, neither could he appropriately make any final demands about the city. The problem of the fortuitous plant—for that matter, the problem of the prosperity of the wicked—was not solved so much as it was *dissolved* by the fact that there was simply no way to climb out of life and bring life as a whole into question, or to bring "God" into question. Did Jonah do well to be angry about the plant? He did? Then surely he should also be grieved over the loss of an entire city. He did not, after all? Then neither was he in a position to make any ultimate judgments about the city.

But if this is more than a perfect squelch or answer which merely "snows" a helpless prophet (as it might first seem), then the whole purpose is to turn Jonah to the question which follows and on which the story ends. "Should not I pity Nineveh, that great city, in which there are more than a hundred and twenty thousand persons who do not know their right hand from their left, and also much cattle?" The last words in the Book of Jonah are a question. The Book of Jonah *means* to leave Jonah, and the reader, with a question—and not merely with a rhetorical question but with an attitude of perpetual questioning. We would miss the very point of that final question by answering it. To say, "No, God should not pity the city," would amount to an attempt to force God or to prejudge ultimate issues; it would amount to choosing destruction for the ignorant if not also the innocent; it would amount to forfeiting the culture actually achieved in the city; it would mean adopting an attitude of "sadness in the presence of a spiritual good"—the good of mercy. On the other hand, simply to say, "Yes, of course God should preserve the city," is to presume equally on the reality of things; it is to tempt God rather than to hear and obey him; it is to be cynical and supine in another way.

Is not the point, rather, that we are to live *with* this ultimate question rather than give an opinionated and stultifying answer to it, that we are to stop being simply argumentative about the city and become attentive again? Is it not exactly by answering this question—by saying, "The city is hopeless," or, "The city will solve all its problems as in the New Jerusalem" —that we *stop* asking other important questions? And is it not exactly by keeping this question open that we keep seeking the answers to all other questions, and that we are ready for surprises of every sort, including those to be unfolded in a new kind of city, provided we are not put off by "confounded" people or plants? Is this not what is meant by the invitation to "watch and wait"—a "watching" which includes more discovery and a "waiting" which includes more action than was ever possible while we were still slow to hear, quick to speak, and quick to anger? (Cf. Jas. 1:19 f.)

III

When the New Testament speaks of "something greater than Jonah" (Matt. 12:41; Luke 11:32) it is not because the question raised by the Book of Jonah found a simple or direct answer in Jesus or in his followers. Actually, that question became heightened, sharpened, and perpetuated in the Gospels. On one occasion, when the people were inclined to interpret what was taking place simply in terms of inherited rules or customary demands, Jesus told a parable of the kingdom which ended remarkably like the story of Jonah. All the workers in the vineyard, those who had borne the heat of the day and those who came only in the last hour, received the same reward —a full day's pay. When the former complained, they were treated with harsh words and a question: "Take what belongs

to you, and go; I choose to give to this last as I give to you. . . .
Or do you begrudge my generosity?" (Matt. 20:14 f.) This
parable meant to "wound from behind" as Jonah was wounded,
to turn its hearers from simply repeating old demands to responding to things in a fresh way. More fundamental than any
human negotiation is an ineluctable gift.

The Gospels spoke of "something greater than Jonah" not
only because they saw in Jesus a new appearance of the question put to Jonah but also because they saw in Jesus something
of the way and the cost of hope in that questioning. They saw
a connection between the "bloody city" and the "blood of
Christ." Jesus did not claim exemption from the judgment
and the oppression befalling his society because he himself was
innocent, because he had not caused them, or because he believed in God. He bore the weight of an injustice and evil not
seen by the best men of his day, while affirming a humanity
and community not acknowledged or sought by them. He bore
the pain of that load for others, even while they helped to
inflict it on him. He bore with disciples who slept, brandished
swords, and fled. He was silent in the judgment hall before
authorities who badgered him and soldiers who brutalized
him. He prayed for those who crucified him: "Father, forgive
them; for they know not what they do" (Luke 23:34). This
was his way of being with naive and violent men. This was
his way of loving the city. This was the price and the hope of
its life.

A New Testament epistle takes up the ensuing question:
Why did persecution and suffering not go out of the way for
followers of Christ? The reason for their suffering was partly,
to be sure, that their behavior and their words were in some
degree different and seemed to be a judgment on other men,
who struck back defensively or sought to show them foolish
and misguided. This was included in the story of the cross,
but it was not the whole story. Jesus Christ actively *accepted*
this load—as the very thing he was called to do. Similarly, his
followers are told: "Do not be surprised at the fiery ordeal
which comes upon you to prove you, as though something

strange were happening to you. But rejoice in so far as you share Christ's sufferings . . . because the spirit of glory and of God rests upon you." Finally, this epistle sets down a most luminous thought: "For the time has come for judgment to begin with the household of God" (I Pet. 4:12-17).

There is a price to be paid for the bloody city, for its manifold opportunities and for all its glitter. There is a price to be paid for technological and social change, when old laws and old institutions do not meet the demands of a new urban day and when work must be done *on* those institutions and laws. There are human needs for which the best and newest organizations and legislation do not provide, requiring much "righteousness which goes beyond the law." An additional price must be paid for the inequities practiced to the third and fourth generation—in schooling, housing, and employment—which new rules of equity in themselves cannot supply. Because people have different needs, there are unique demands written into every concrete human encounter—rules of equity describe only how people must all be treated alike. Someone must be ready and willing to pay this extra price, even if that price is raised by the reactions of those who refuse to pay it. Someone must be ready to say not merely "Why me?" but "To this was I called." There must be some who make it a point to ask with each new day: Which practices from the past are no longer viable and must therefore be given up? What is the new obedience which must be taken up if changes taking place in the society are to be for the better rather than the worse? Some will have to see the times when a life must still be offered for the city, occasionally in the course of keeping order, but no less in the course of waking people up to the injustices being enforced within it. This is the price of the bloody city. This is how the city is to be loved. This is what it means to be not only an inhabitant but a citizen, and not only a citizen but a man!

Here was something which Nineveh, for all its power and glitter, did not clearly understand. It was something which might never be fully understood or accepted in Nineveh, even if judgment were to be averted a hundred times. What with all those people who did not know their right hands from their left! And what with all those cattle which looked at what was going on the way any cow looks at a new gate!

IV

American cities have become like Ninevehs. The economic power and attraction of our big cities must be recognized in every small town and hamlet. The American nation has become a Nineveh on the world scene. Its economic and military power must be reckoned with by virtually every country in the world. American cities and the American nation have been regarded, moreover, as living with naive assumptions. This judgment is only partially the result of envy. Any nation which began as this one did, which has enjoyed seemingly limitless frontiers and unparalleled good fortune, is likely to carry along uncriticized assumptions concerning its virtue as well as concerning its use of power.

In helping to colonize and subdue a new land in which labor was needed and prized, a man could forget his past prison term in Europe; a Wyatt Earp could be a marshal in one town and wanted for murder in the next. In conducting a revolution and building new institutions, the founding fathers did not have to overthrow the culture of their own fathers and grandfathers, as in other modern revolutions, only that of the Indian nations which, though often highly cultivated, were regarded as less than human. The American Indians were refused access to the white man's courts, were paid to bring in one another's scalps, and were subjected to virtual genocide, unparalleled in modern history with the exception of Hitler's attempt on the Jews. Such a policy which "delivered up a whole people" called forth the harshest visions of the prophet Amos—but it has seldom seriously disturbed the American dream.

American industry was built on the backs of immigrant labor, often chained to machines for twelve hours a day, six days a week—but such facts could be overlooked so long as the immigrant himself was able to save his money and move up, or buy a wagon and move out. The growing economy of this nation afforded the greatest instance in modern history of slave labor, but those who profited could tell themselves that the blacks were not really human—just as others could later pretend that a bloody, fraternal war, or an Emancipation Proclamation, or certain legal gains in civil rights, had made it all right again. Western railroads were built on the bodies of Oriental laborers whose descendants have been fenced out by immigration laws and fenced in by wartime alien laws as whites have never been. The marvel is that our nation could emerge from all this with a sense of "innocence" still intact. This sense has been fortified by easy expansion and decisive victories in our experience with other nations, if we begin counting after the War of 1812 and do not probe the partisan rhetoric attending the most recent warfare in Korea and Vietnam.

The combination of "innocence" and "power" is violence. A modern American historian describes this nation as "entrapped by history in the ethos of violence." The white hats, fast guns, and pure vengeance of the American Western may be nothing more than harmless folklore, but violence also marks much other popular American entertainment and much American news. Is there no connection between the alleged "American naiveté" and the manner of this nation's participation in earlier wars—its first standing aloof and then entering with massive bombings and demands for total surrender? Having a giant's strength, we are always tempted to use it like a giant.

We are, perhaps, speaking more soberly today. But the squalor in American cities is still overlooked by many on the basis of the unreviewed assumption that the poor are able to "move up or move out"—a possibility which is undercut both by an old racism and by new developments in agriculture, industry, and the professions. Stirrings within other countries are still methodically opposed in the name of our "vital interests," which we readily assume are their best interests as well. Patriots within those countries who disagree or look to other alliances are sometimes bought and sometimes shot, with our representatives looking the other way. If we consider the facts of seething discontent within our cities and independent stirrings within other nations, together with the facts of mounting reaction and repressive measures, we may find ourselves beginning to ask not merely "whether" but "when."

To an unreconstructed Jonah, it might seem that the cup is almost full, that no nation with so much blood on its hands, and so many illusions on its lips, should have another chance. But for any Jonah whose own naiveté and will for violence have been repeatedly exposed, who has himself been repeatedly reclaimed by surprise and joy, such judgments turn into questions: Does he do well to be angry? Ought not God to pity Nineveh? Are we awake to *everything* that is going on: to the new voices combining self-criticism and hope, to the new discussions concerning the use of power at home and abroad, to the new attention to the poverty and powerlessness of the poor, and to the new forms of economic and political organization in developing cities at home as well as in developing nations abroad? What might it mean for other countries and for our own cities if this nation outgrew its illusions of innocence and omnipotence? Are we bent on tasks of discussion and responsive reorganization in view of that possibility?

There is no simple answer to the question with which we put down the Book of Jonah, such that one could write that answer down and forget the question. The answer lies in taking up the question afresh with each new day—not on the assumption that everything is certain to come out all right, nor on the assumption that the grapes of wrath must soon overrun the streets, but in the watchfulness and responsiveness of faith.

It is too late to turn our backs on the modern city and too early to sing a song which calls only for burning. The word— and song—for now calls us all to turn our faces to the city and to burn the midnight oil!

The Temptations of Jesus:

Of Seductions Old and New

Then Jesus was led up by the Spirit into the wilderness to be tempted by the devil. And he fasted forty days and forty nights, and afterward he was hungry. And the tempter came and said to him, "If you are the Son of God, command these stones to become loaves of bread." But he answered, "It is written,

'Man shall not live by bread alone,

but by every word that proceeds from the mouth of God.'"

Then the devil took him to the holy city, and set him on the pinnacle of the temple, and said to him, "If you are the Son of God, throw yourself down; for it is written,

'He will give his angels charge of you,'

and

'On their hands they will bear you up,

lest you strike your foot against a stone.'"

Jesus said to him, "Again it is written, 'You shall not tempt the Lord your God.'" Again, the devil took him to a very high mountain, and showed him all the kingdoms of the world and the glory of them; and he said to him, "All these I will give you, if you will fall down and worship me." Then Jesus said to him, "Begone, Satan! for it is written,

'You shall worship the Lord your God

and him only shall you serve.'"

Then the devil left him, and behold, angels came and ministered to him.

—Matthew 4:1–11 -

FOUR

Being Led to See
Behind the Scenes

*Then Jesus was led up by the Spirit into the wilderness
to be tempted by the devil.*—Matthew 4:1

WE HAVE BEEN TALKING,
and learning from the Scriptures to talk, about a "sleep"
which may befall us all and which may become a particularly
deep sleep in the case of believers. Our next text distinguishes
three *kinds* of sleep one may fall into or choose. In the first
two, if we may say so, we are seduced into bed or into sleep;
in the third we are no longer seduced but willing.

Now, of course, people who are sleeping don't really know
it and there is something strange about any attempt to make
them know it. There is something odd about asking someone
whether he is asleep, though we do sometimes shake somebody
gleefully and say, "Wake up and tell us whether you're asleep!"
If he is sleeping, he does not answer at all; and if he does
answer, he couldn't possibly be sleeping—at least not anymore. Something similar could be said about seduction: if you
don't know you are being seduced, then you could hardly say
that you *are*; and if you do know you are being seduced, then
it could hardly be called "seduction."

The story of Jesus' temptations in the Gospel of Matthew
is devised to bring all of this out: to show why people are

asleep, if they are, and to suggest what kind of seductions may have gotten them into bed or why they have chosen to close their eyes. Some, of course, may come awake in the process and may even be able to tell us about their dreams, and that would be all to the good. But those who are not awake are not likely to be disturbed by this simple story at all.

I

Scholars who have made historical studies of this text describe it as similar in some ways to the "hermetic" stories told in certain groups during the first centuries. These were stories which enfolded a fundamental secret in such a way as to conceal it from some while imparting it to others, as an underground group might seek to communicate with sympathizers without arousing the notice of others in the crowd, or as parents sometimes try to communicate without alerting their children, and vice versa. Those who catch the secret in the story may be trusted because they are "in the know," while those who do not catch it are none the wiser. This kind of discourse, through which one either comes to the light or remains in darkness but which is not intended merely to impart a piece of ordinary information to all, is frequently mentioned in the Gospel of John. Dostoevski saw such a fundamental significance in this story of Jesus' temptations: "The statement of those three questions was itself the miracle," says the Grand Inquisitor in Ivan's long speech, "for in those three temptations the whole subsequent history of mankind is foretold . . . and in them are united all the unsolved contradictions of human nature."

In this respect, the story of the three temptations is a distilled essence of something which is frequently at work in Matthew's Gospel. The theme of this Gospel, if one were to be stated, is that Jesus of Nazareth was, in spite of certain differing expectations in the people of his day, the Messiah of Israel. And yet the Gospel does not often say this in so many words and does not intend merely to bring us to say

52

this or to agree that this was so. It wishes, at the same time, to impart a surprising new meaning which is enfolded in the discovery that Jesus is that Messiah. From the outset, this Gospel lets no opportunity pass for *suggesting* to us that Jesus is the one who now carries the mission of Israel, or for letting that picture lodge itself in our minds. Jesus is born in the city of David, and Micah's prophecy about Bethlehem is duly cited. Matthew includes the story of the Magi, told with an eye to the psalms about kings coming from afar with gifts. The slaughter of the innocents recalls the weeping in Ramah of which Jeremiah wrote, and the return of the holy family from Egypt serves to recall the Exodus itself and the words of Hosea: "Out of Egypt I called my son" (Hos. 11:1). Jesus passes through the waters of baptism in the wilderness and, lest this image escape us, a title is put over the entire scene, "This is my beloved Son, with whom I am well pleased," words which refer almost unmistakably to Israel's songs about its king and its servant (Ps. 2:7; Isa. 42:1). Jesus then spends forty days in the wilderness, as Moses and Elijah did and as Israel itself was disciplined for forty years as a "firstborn son" in the wilderness (Exod. 4:22). It is no coincidence that all the words spoken by Jesus in reply to the temptations are from Deuteronomy, and in particular from the "farewell address" of Moses which refers to Israel's testing in the wilderness. Jesus will go on to give a renewed law to a renewed people of God "on the mount"—and the Gospel of Matthew has only begun.

To say the least, we are allowed to catch the notion that Jesus is the one to whom the faith of Israel has pointed. But Matthew does not want us to miss, through a too-ready acceptance, the full significance of saying that. That Jesus should have been the Messiah entailed something of a surprise in terms of widespread expectations. He did not, after all, get on a horse, drive out the Romans, and reign in Jerusalem in the sight of the nations—as those who remembered David thought the Messiah would do. He had not come on the clouds of heaven, as the Son of Man was expected to do. He was born, he suffered, he died in disgrace on a Roman cross. There is a discovery waiting to be made: not merely *that* Jesus is the Messiah, but *what* it is to be the Messiah and what it means to *see* that Jesus is the Messiah. This disclosure includes nothing less than a new understanding of what it is (or how it is) to be a man—a Palestinian Jewish man, to be sure, but also a Gentile man, or a man anywhere at all!

"To you it has been given to know the secrets of the kingdom of heaven," Jesus says to his disciples in Matthew's Gospel, "but to [others] it has not been given . . . because seeing they do not see, and hearing they do not hear, nor do they understand" (Matt. 13:11, 13). These words are themselves hard to understand, but the story of Jesus' temptations does function in that manner. It means to clarify our entire self-understanding or point of view, not merely to add something to our store of information. Some who hear the story are left unmoved or simply puzzled by it, and they go on playing their accustomed roles. Others who hear the story are "taken" and enlightened by it; they are led behind the scenes to see the dressing room in which their roles have been devised; they are ready to follow new prompting when they step out again before the lights.

II

The opening sentence itself is a puzzler: Jesus is "led up by the Spirit into the wilderness to be tempted by the devil." Each phrase, in fact, is strange—unless these words have been worn so smooth that we simply slide over them. If they do seem odd, it is not only because we are separated by many years from the composition of this text, though that complicates our task of understanding it, but also because a strangeness is written into the very texture of the text.

Jesus is being "led by the Spirit." He is responding to something, though not to promptings ordinarily described. He is not working on a project which he devised for himself, nor is he off on a whim. He is not going to the wilderness to conduct geophysical explorations, nor is he going to test his ability to survive alone in the bush, either of which purposes would be assignable to familiar causes. Following a whim would have been, in one sense, the most mechanical kind of following. The word "spirit," with whatever other meaning it carries, always signifies freedom from ordinary causes. How is one "led" in such a way as to characterize human freedom? We are going to get a picture of a free man in action, of how a man responds when he is acting most freely.

Jesus is being led "into the wilderness." We do not ordinarily think of the wilderness as a place of temptation. We are more likely to speak of "the temptations of the city." One of the catchy lines in *My Fair Lady* expresses a common notion that temptation is most likely to take place where there are enjoyable things at hand: "The Lord above gave liquor for temptation." We usually imagine, rightly or wrongly, that monks and hermits go to the wilderness to *escape* temptation, and we are amused by stories of Saint Anthony's being tempted even in the desert by visions of dancing girls no less distracting than the real thing. Yet Jesus is being led into the wilderness *to be tempted,* not to escape temptation. He is being led to see a kind of temptation which might otherwise escape his attention, perhaps precisely *because* of the more customary meanings of "temptation." He is being led to face an issue he might miss so long as he is engaged only in self-imposed or generally recognized tests of character.

This is not to say that the moral tests we ordinarily speak of are unimportant. Everyone has to choose between present and future goods when they come into conflict. Such powers or habits cannot be developed without practice; accordingly, we learn to identify and even welcome situations requiring them. Boy scouts talk about doing a "good deed" every day. Ethical culturists seek to develop principled involvement in larger social issues. "Every day in every way I am getting better and better" expresses a time-honored understanding that moral improvement is possible by cultivating habits of referring to funded rules of behavior. If such a phrase seems quaint to us today, it is because we are aware of more complicated or unique circumstances in which inherited rules do not apply in a simply wooden way, and in which *we* might become wooden to apply them in that way; it is because we wish to develop a *more* discriminating judgment, not because we no longer wish to practice judgment at all. No one expects to live without any tests of discernment or will. On the contrary, we are invited and intrigued by such situations and do not want them to be simplified by standard responses. This urbane development prompted W. H. Auden's prayer of the bored housewife: "Lord, lead us into temptation for our sakes."

But none of this quite focuses the meaning of Jesus' temptation in the *wilderness*. In the passion story, Jesus did not tell his disciples to pray for judgment, courage, or willpower in temptation; he told them to pray that they might not enter into temptation. The very phrase "*fall* into temptation" points to a kind of test which we do not choose on the basis of our previous lights or developed strength. In the wilderness there was little to test Jesus in the ordinary sense of "testing" and little use for moral prescriptions or the willpower to apply them. Something even more fundamental was to come into question.

The "wilderness" is not merely a strange environment; it is a place in which one has lost all familiar landmarks. Perhaps only one who has actually been "lost in the wilderness," in the forest, or at sea, without any of the environmental supports he has known from infancy, can fully appreciate this significance of the word. Everything by which one customarily gets his bearings, by which one feels at home and enjoys familiar responses, has vanished. This picture is used again and again in the Scriptures to get at the nature of faith, at an affirmation often concealed by habitual or formal behavior. Jesus' temptations take place in a setting in which every conventional meaning of "good" has fallen out of the picture. This is the biblical way of raising an issue which may in actuality always be present but which may not in fact be recognized so long as one acts on the basis of familiar customs and concepts.

These, then, are initial clues calling attention to the unique issue in Jesus' temptation: his being "led by the Spirit," not by some ordinary project or problem, "into the wilderness" where he is separated from every commonplace understanding or support. These phrases may serve to recall other familiar sayings about how "every earthly prop gives way," how "strength of our own does not avail," and how "our striving would be losing." Our cultivated understanding and developed strength are useless in the temptation we are trying to understand; and they may also (to make the matter clearer) become worse than useless. One complains, on the basis of his accustomed ideas of fairness and personal worth: "Why should this be happening to me?"; "Why should *I* have to . . ."; "If you *are* the Son of God, why should *you* . . .?" That is the kind of temptation against which we pray in the Lord's Prayer: "Lead us not into temptation." We pray in this petition, Luther said, that we should not be deceived or seduced into "unbelief" or "despair." At the base of our humanity is something more fundamental than shared morality and our willingness to observe it.

Oscar Wilde once wrote, no doubt facetiously, "I can resist anything but temptation." He was dead-right with respect to the temptation before us. The question is whether we can recognize the issue in this temptation, one which bears not merely on our adopted standards or our derived choices but on a final basis of our own choosing which is not here described as conventional or chosen at all.

III

". . . To be tempted by the devil." This phrase seems the most strange of all. Some of us are cocking a left eye as if to say, "Surely we don't believe there is a devil anymore"; and some are cocking a right eye as if to say, "Now we'll see whether we believe the old truths anymore"; and some of us are arching both eyebrows as if to say, "Now we'll get the latest solution to the question of evil."

The word "devil" belongs in the same class as those other difficult words in our text, "Spirit" and "wilderness," and that is where we will seek its meaning. When we speak of "evil" actions, as when we speak of "good" actions, we do not customarily offer "natural" explanations (in the sense of physical or psychological causes) for them. "Good" and "evil" describe actions insofar as they are based on reflection concerning what is most to be sought in any situation. Often we distinguish actions in which such deliberation takes place from more automatic responses or instrumental calculations as "free" actions. If we have described "good" actions of this sort as "being led by the Spirit," how shall we describe "evil" actions of this sort except as being led by another spirit, "the devil"? If authentic faith or valid affirmation underlying human action was at issue in the wilderness, how shall we describe unfaith or bad faith except in terms of seduction or willful blindness for other than "natural" causes? The Bible customarily describes faith as "given" or "taken out of one's heart," and not as manufactured or acquired. The devil in our story does not so much explain evil or account for evil as help us to define it.

The role of Satan or the "devil" in the Scriptures is a diversified one, yet it may usually be seen to bear on this point. Through most of the Old Testament, the word "Satan" refers to a functionary whose work had a constructive relationship, though an inversely constructive one, to faith in Jahweh. Satan was an accuser or plaintiff (Zech. 3:1; Ps. 109:6, 20–29) whose accusations served the cause of genuine faithfulness and obedience to the Lord God of Israel. Jahweh himself is said to have raised up "Satans" against Solomon. The "accuser" in the Book of Job is one of the "sons of God" who serves as a kind of attorney-general for heaven, going about the earth and seeing whether faith is all that it is meant to be. On this occasion he raises a question concerning the apparently righteous and pious Job: "Does Job fear God for nought?" God himself gives Job into the hand of the accuser in stages (1:11; 2:4), until everything is taken from him except his physical life and his nagging wife. At some point it is to be made clear whether the faith of Job is authentic or not, or if he is to come to a more authentic faith—and in this way the story lays bare the very nature of faith for its readers. In all this, the accuser is still somehow in the service of God, performing a kind of left-hand function of testing fidelity, exposing infidelity, and perhaps also of executing a kind of refinement or nemesis on bad faith.

Between the Old and New Testaments, Satan came to be described more and more as an outright enemy who deliberately opposed God's will for the world. In the New Testament the devil is such a deceiver intent on darkness rather than on light. He no longer runs to and fro on the earth merely checking the quality of people's faith but prowls about as a roaring lion seeking someone to devour (I Pet. 5:8). He is "prince of this world" and "god of this world" (Luke 4:6; II Cor. 4:4). There is a battle between the "kingdom of God" and the "kingdom of Satan." But a crucial meeting, and reversal, takes place in Jesus. Satan shows up inevitably at the beginning and the end of Jesus' ministry, and he is active in the betrayal. But this time—eminently—faith, not unfaith, is revealed, and all the subtleties of temptation are exposed. In a figure used by Luther, the devil saw Jesus as his prize, snapped at the bait, and was pulled out of the water for all to see. His effects may still be disastrous (one is wise to note how hardened structures enforce evil in the world), but his power is now, in the light of Christ, an "empty show." It is precisely his attacks which serve to reveal the kingdom of God that Jesus proclaimed, for they help to clarify the function of faith and to produce "true men." Precisely in his most bitter and most inimical attack on Jesus the devil turns out to be "God's devil" after all.

The story of the temptations beams its light at the most fundamental attitude at work in our actions, an attitude which is usually concealed (often from ourselves) but which is nevertheless effective in outward actions and which has cumulative consequences in the world. For lack of clarity in this matter, we fall without reflection on the "next thing," whether it be a "worldly" or a "religious" thing; we become like lemmings, walking on our own legs into the sea. Even *with* clarity, we may despair of other men or of ourselves and choose simply to make life safer or more comfortable for ourselves and other lemmings. The story of the temptations wishes to make these ever present perils plain to us and to show another possibility in one who walked on and off the field a free man.

"Spirit," "tempted," "wilderness," and "devil" stand as strange words at the beginning of our story. May they not, partly for this very reason, point to convictions underlying our actions which are less explicit for us but which are no less important for that reason? May they not help us who are busy in unprecedented situations as scientists and technicians, in service professions, and as citizens, to ask a question entailed in all such activities—the question of how to direct them in a fully human and fully responsive way? Are we willing to take that chance, to follow Christ into the wilderness to witness a temptation which might transfigure every problem? The people of Israel were disciplined for forty years in the wilderness before taking up the new challenges of land and society. If eyes are newly opened in the wilderness today, what will they begin to see in the modern city?

Our story makes a promise: being in the wilderness with Christ makes it possible both to see the fundamental issues more clearly and to face them adequately. But there will be no surprise if we cock or wink an eye or even keep our eyes closed. Our story knows that people who are accustomed to thinking in terms of competencies, customs, and superstitions find the question of faith strange. It is completely serious about seduction in the world, and it knows about the sleep of sorrow.

FIVE

Secular Seductions

And he fasted forty days and forty nights, and afterward he was hungry. And the tempter came and said to him, "If you are the Son of God, command these stones to become loaves of bread." But he answered, "It is written, 'Man shall not live by bread alone, but by every word that proceeds from the mouth of God.'"—Matthew 4:2–4

I

WE HAVE ALL BEEN WARNED by the first sentence of our story that it has unusual designs on us. The temptations which follow speak right out of the human condition, out of actual human engagements in the world. But they are not resisted simply by means of the calculations or efforts needed to manipulate the special objects of those engagements; they must be resisted by looking, at the same time, to purposes or possibilities beyond them. This is signaled in the narrative of the first temptation by an art as subtle and self-concealing as the temptation itself. Jesus has fasted for forty days and forty nights and is famished. There is no need more basic or universal than hunger and no demand more immediate or legitimate than a demand for bread. Yet in this story something overrules or subsumes even this most fundamental demand. The question is, *what* validly does so? To what is Jesus listening besides hunger and to what is he looking besides bread?

The famished condition of Jesus is important in setting the scene. Mark's Gospel describes Jesus' temptations as continuing for forty days, but Matthew wants us to see this temptation as coming *after* the forty days. We are to see the man Jesus as weak and empty in the face of this temptation, without ordinary "inner" reasons or resources for meeting it. In one sense, Jesus' "inner voices" help to tempt him. When the seducer says, "If you are the Son of God," this is not to be understood as raising a question concerning Jesus' *ability* to do the thing requested—as improbable as commanding stones to become loaves of bread might seem to us and as much as we might like to see that tested. That kind of ability or power is not really being questioned in this text. Elsewhere in the Gospel, Jesus does perform miracles, including one with bread (and sometimes he refuses to do so); even false Messiahs were said to work miracles. The question was not so much whether Jesus *could* satisfy his hunger in these circumstances as whether he *should* do so. The challenge was not, "Let's see whether you really are the Son of God"; it bore rather on what it *meant* to be the Son of God, on *how* the Son of God would act. The sublety of the seducer lay in his seizing on the very conviction and prerogative of Jesus: "Since you are the Son of God, why should *you* of all people have to suffer in this way, or suffer so long, or (in any case) suffer any longer?" It was not Jesus' own conviction of his sonship which was being questioned; that conviction all by itself, and by its very strength, helped to pose the question.

Jesus' reply, accordingly, was not a demonstration with stones to show that he really was the Son of God. It was rather a non-demonstration which exemplified what was entailed in living as the Son of God. His reply was, in effect: "Exactly *because* I am the Son of God I do not at this moment turn stones into bread; I live by every word as it proceeds from the mouth of God." The particular word for those days in the wilderness was that Jesus should be thinking not about his private needs or rights but about other men and his calling to them; and while that word usually includes eating bread, it also focuses on further demands which should not be forgotten even when one's body is clamoring for bread. The words which Jesus speaks are from the Book of Deuteronomy, specifically from its reflective understanding of Israel's testing as a "firstborn son" in the wilderness. Israel was always to remember how the Lord God had led it during those forty years in the wilderness, testing it to see what was in its heart; Israel was never to forget how it had been disciplined by hunger and manna to know that "man does not live by bread alone, but by every word that proceeds from the mouth of God." All this was training for life in a good land, in which the people would have plenty of bread and in which the hills would be filled with iron and copper (Deut. 8:2-10). Israel would be ready for bread by its own hand, even for a civilization of abundance, when it had learned to live by *everything* that proceeds out of the mouth of the Lord.

Many modern seductions begin with words such as, "Since we're human," "Why not be a little human?" "After all, we're only human." Such seductions can be resisted only by saying, "Because we're human." The question arises, What does it mean to be human? Or, more precisely, How does one act or respond in a fully human way?

II

We often think of becoming a man or of developing our manhood in terms of developing certain moral as well as physical powers within ourselves. We speak of such "virtues" in the abstract, and do not always specify what they are virtuous *for*. Freedom can be simply defined as having the power to do what we wish to do, the power to achieve chosen ends. Since this includes the power to deny oneself immediate, lesser desires in pursuit of more distant, greater ones, we speak about the virtue of self-denial or willpower. We are inclined to see the story of Jesus' temptations in that way: here was a young man at the outset of his career developing his physical stamina, his self-discipline, and his ability to stick it out just as long as he had decided to do.

But there is much in the story of Jesus' temptations to indicate that such virtues in themselves are not the entire issue. For one thing, Jesus is described as being *led* into the wilderness; this was not an excursion he deliberately undertook for the sake of developing his moral muscle. For another thing, the crucial temptations take place *after* forty days of fasting, that is, after the canonical period which might have been chosen for self-development, and after he had learned whatever he wanted to learn by way of self-development or self-discipline. Finally, his very words make clear that the point of it all was something other than developing powers within himself which would enable him to do what he chose to do; the point was rather to develop a responsiveness to demands outside himself which might enable him to choose correctly, to do things he might not otherwise have chosen to do. Self-denial in itself (choosing during Lent, say, to forego tobacco or Julie Christie movies) is a misleading form of faithful "watchfulness," unless it is a self-discipline adopted in the interest of responding to actual demands and opportunities we have been inclined to ignore. But then a better discipline would be one of actually trying to name such opportunities and of being at the place of such demands, day after day—which would turn out not to be "special" training at all.

The point of the first temptation is not that it is good to deny oneself pleasure, and neither is it that it is good to accept pain. Periods of suffering are indeed said to develop virtues such as patience or endurance, and they may be viewed as schooling for life. But in Jesus' temptation something further is at issue. This is a suffering which continues even after the time for ordinary learning is over. It is not accepted because physical preservation or social enhancement require it. It is not "right" because established rules require it, or because social or religious customs prescribe it. Yet it *is* required. Jesus refers to requirements which may be heard in, but also beside and beyond those of familiar appetites, customs, and institutions. "Man does not live by bread alone, but by *every* word that proceeds from the mouth of God."

To define temptation simply in terms of "self-denial" might result in an absurd unresponsiveness to pleasurable things. To define temptation simply in terms of "accepting suffering" might result in an absurd weakening of our physical capacities or an absurd neglect of health measures. Worst of all, either notion might result in failure to see larger opportunities and perils when they are actually set before us. And both attitudes, as we shall see, run right into the teeth of the second temptation, which *seeks* to lead us into a denial of the needs and laws of the body in the interest of some separate "spiritual" ambition or desire.

III

The first temptation finds new expression and new subtlety in a society of abundance. An affluent society has come into being amid endemic poverty at home and fearsome hunger abroad. Even in the United States one-fourth of the people live below the "poverty line" as usually defined. The number of the nation's poor has not diminished significantly since Franklin Roosevelt's shocking announcement in the thirties: "One-third of a nation ill-housed, ill-clad, ill-nourished." What *has* improved (more through national defense than domestic measures) is the "average income," not the lot of the poor who tend to get lost under averages. This is to say nothing of the rest of the world in which, if current trends continue, there will be a billion people literally starving in 1970.

It is a hopeful sign that the "invisible poor" are being seen today as never before. That is partly the result of a changed technology and economy. There is no need and no excuse for the poverty prevailing in our cities and rural areas. The old excuses about the unwillingness, laziness, or unworthiness of the poor have been called into question by new studies of the mechanics or "cycles" of poverty. People are not hungry simply because they are lazy; they are also lazy because they are hungry, and because they have limited opportunities. Students drop out of lower schools when there is little hope of going on to higher schools and little access to acceptable jobs without such credentials. The ghetto dweller is not likely to save his money so long as he must pay more for everything he buys and much more interest for any available funds for investment. He is not likely to go into business while small business has a high mortality rate and big business has room for him only at the bottom. In one sense his most "rational" investment is the numbers game, even though it keeps him broke. There is a simple contradiction between saying, on the one hand, that the Negro is poor because he is lazy, and, on the other hand, that the white has a right to every advantage; or between saying that the Negro is inferior, and expecting him to behave more virtuously than other people have ever behaved. Above all, there is a rising vitality in the poor themselves as they begin to inspect such contradictions and as economic capacities are pumped to them by the media from every side.

There is today a legitimate cry for bread. Words offered in place of bread, even moral and religious words, are becoming more and more suspect. The poor are learning to see through promises of "pie in the sky" spoken by people who have pie in their grasp. There is little use in being told that you have to work for everything you get by someone who opposes the minimum wage and whose table is supplied in whole or in part by dividends from machines he never saw. The assertion that "man does not live by bread alone" loses some of its plausibility when it is made by those who are full to those who are hungry. It could also take on newly powerful meanings among the poor which the rich did not intend.

There is a rising cry today which begins, "Since we are men. . . ." Freedom from hunger, the right to bread, the right to live in dignity and not on a dole—because we are men! Notable economists have proposed a guaranteed annual income for all citizens as a matter of national policy and human right. A machine economy, which increases production while reducing labor, is said to make this measure both necessary and possible. It is needed at once, many argue, to prevent civil disorders in the cities.

Let us agree that there is a need for some adequate program

of this kind in the future, and then ask our question. Is there not a temptation lurking near this demand and proposal with respect to bread, a temptation to offer, or to accept, this measure as a pacifier, rather than as a means to participation and power? There was a time when the poor were exploited for their labor. Might they not become newly exploited as customers and clients? Every morning armies of professional workers enter deprived neighborhoods, and every evening they leave them again, taking the rewards for their services both ways. Michael Harrington, who taught us all in *The Other America* to see the "invisible poor," has more recently written a chapter on "the decadence of the poor." He imagines a time when the poor will be fed, housed, entertained, and counseled, and he asks: Where then will lie the springs of social reform? Beyond the need for bread, is there not a need for men to speak, to decide, to act, to serve—to share in making the decisions and in shaping the institutions which affect their lives? If the procedures or institutions of a society do not allow the poor to speak or serve in this way, must they not form enterprises and organizations of their own by which to do so? Must they not refuse to be dissuaded by any offers or threats dealing only in bread? Must they not use their buying power for economic development and political freedom?

This is not far from the point of the first temptation, a temptation to choose the "bread which perishes" without giving attention to the "bread which endures." In addition to seeking economic security, a man must also take up political tasks. But even these are not immune to temptation. Social and political movements themselves offer seductions. "Human dignity" is their rallying cry and sometimes it is given as their goal. The seduction is subtle because without participation in public decisions and actions a man cannot respond in a fully human way. Yet one does not join a political movement in order to *become* a man. One joins because he *is* a man. Otherwise he is likely to be a poor worker or to be disappointed by his work —when typing letters and licking postage stamps day after day seem less than humanizing. "Manhood" is not, strictly

67

speaking, produced *by* politicial movements; a man is one who works *in* such movements and who joins new movements. Even social and political leaders can become tempters who say, "After all, we're only human," and need to hear in reply, "*Because* we're human."

This demand may seem to place too great a burden on the poor. The Grand Inquisitor saw it as too severe to gain general acceptance: "Dost thou not know that the ages will pass and humanity will proclaim by the lips of their sages that there is no crime and no sin; there is only hunger?" The masses would always be ready to lay their freedom at the feet of established leaders and say, "Make us your slaves, but feed us." If Jesus had taken a more limited view of human potentialities, if he had been willing to serve as a religious or political demagogue, the people might have fared better with him and he with them. To such reasonings there is sometimes no direct answer except this word: "It is written, 'Man shall not live by bread alone, but by every word that proceeds from the mouth of God.'"

If this reply makes heavy demands upon the poor, what does it require of the wealthy and the established? They are certainly no less devoted to "bread," and are often equally reluctant to respond to larger demands. They are accustomed to asking of every new job, "What does it pay?" and of every new public policy, "What will it cost?" These are indeed valid questions, but not the kind which will lead them beyond well-established institutions and services. "I have to think of my family" is a phrase often heard from hard-working householders, and an appropriate one. But does not everything depend on *what* one thinks of his family and on what one wants his family to think? Who leaves a greater legacy, the man who seeks only to provide his family with every security and comfort and to shield it from the world, or the man who sojourns in the land of promise with his sons, resting on no foundations his own hands have laid? What policies might wealthy men pursue if they "look forward to the city which has foundations, whose builder and maker is God"? (Heb. 11:10.)

IV

A new science and technology are producing a new kind of city, even while we are standing amid the decrepit structures of an older one. As surely as industrialization produced the city we know, in spite of every protest along the way, new specialized sciences and technologies, and new machines combining self-repairing with self-programming capabilities, are producing another city or metropolis or megalopolis or whatever we're going to call it. The question arises whether there are any seductions, like that of the first temptation, attending this development in our society.

Technology is a distinctly appropriate human activity, and it is conducive to valuable human ends. The grinding labor which consumed the time and energy of many human lives in previous generations was not necessarily conducive to the "humanness" of anyone. Television makes communication more rapid and direct, more vivid and universal, than print ever could. If problems have become more complex, problem-solving operations are also faster and more accurate than ever before. There is now a technological hope that man will at last be able to subdue the earth and the sea and the new realms of space, that he will heal all the sick and cause all baskets to overflow.

Many are more cautious. Once it took twenty-four man-hours to produce a Ford engine block; now it takes 14.6 minutes. How will we provide for the vast relocations and dislocations of labor which such facts portend? How will we provide for all those extra Fords in our future, when highways are already eating up the surfaces of our cities and fumes are already filling the air we breathe? What can stem such tides so long as the economy itself depends on large enterprises, which in turn require large-scale planning and allocation of resources and which therefore pour out their messages from the media every day? *One* kind of response, to be sure, is a foredoomed attempt to turn back the clock. Unemployed men declare automation their enemy; laborers seize the present moment to drive hard bargains for themselves, if not for their sons. But there is no turning back the tide. Corporate, machine production is a fact of life. If one company or nation does not proceed with it, another will. It would probably prove demeaning, in any case, to go on performing a job one knew a machine could be doing as well or better.

Yet is it not exactly the peril of the first temptation simply to surrender to the new technology, either in enthusiasm for the bread it supplies or in despair over its inevitability—simply to stand in a growing line with our tin cups in hand, waiting to see what the new day will bring? Then, in a way Emerson never dreamed, "things are in the saddle and they ride mankind." The problems are massive, but does not the reply to the first temptation prohibit us from resting with the problems of production, and demand that we also take up ensuing societal problems? Must we not apply as much effort to facilitating societal decisions as we have to distributing products? Might we not apply some of the same technology to developing interaction between planners and affected people, to disseminating information, debating issues, offering proposals, and registering votes?

We might prefer simply to entrust our future to the decisions made by the technocrats, producers, and distributors themselves. The competence of American business is well known. Businessmen are noted for their moral insistence, self-discipline, and willpower. It is customary, in view of changing circumstances, for large corporations to consider themes like "self-renewal" and to include on their agendas not only increased worker benefits but improved public relations and expanded service projects as well. There is a limit, however, to what one may expect from such intramural efforts on behalf of society. One cannot expect any business to pursue ends which conflict with its own profit or power; in so doing it would diminish or forfeit its power to serve. One cannot expect an advertiser to take the irrelevant but attractive beauty out of his copy, for if he doesn't use her, his competitor might. What *may* be expected is that those advertisers will seek a common agreement or accept certain public controls which would govern them both. But even that is likely to prove insufficient if government is not kept independent of business, a difficult task in view of their interdependence. Business is business, but for that very reason there are political tasks both of encouraging and regulating business, as well as further tasks of keeping government itself responsive to the people.

There are seductions in the very competencies of the present age. One is tempted to think only of the "bread" they supply, rather than of the human life which is to be supplied. Faith means living "by *every* word as it proceeds from the mouth of God" and this means listening for a word concerning every new competence and its role in the society, as well as for new words concerning the roles of old ones. The seeds of hope are found in such attentiveness to things, not in wishful dreaming.

So far as new technologies bring new possibilities, so far as the basic problems now confronting society are solved, the "proceeding" word will summon enjoyment—the very enjoyment which comes when one combines a sense of gift with a sense of achievement, and which includes a "sacrifice of thanksgiving." Those who receive their daily bread with thanksgiving, including new forms of bread which come daily, will also be ready to deal that bread to the hungry, and to help their society do so. Otherwise, rich or poor, they will eat the bread of sorrows.

To the extent that technological change brings dislocation and inequities at certain points in the society, the word will require something more. So far from merely scrambling for one's own share of the new bread, or holding for dear life to one's old share, it will require taking up the new burdens brought by change. It will require seeking adequate provisions for all who are adversely affected by the change and for all who could benefit by it, even when such measures are resisted. This will come as no surprise to those who find "true manhood" in Jesus' reply to the first temptation and who remember how he went from victory in this temptation to a cross.

Will it be thanksgiving or a cross? Or curiously, in every case, both! Are we people who have little day-by-day use for either of these words, "thanksgiving" or "cross"? If *that* is the case, is it because the story of the temptations is too old to mean very much to us anymore? Or is it because we ourselves have been seduced into bed by the first temptation which came along?

SIX

Religious Seductions

> *Then the devil took him to the holy city, and set him on the pinnacle of the temple, and said to him, "If you are the Son of God, throw yourself down; for it is written, 'He will give his angels charge of you,' and 'On their hands they will bear you up, lest you strike your foot against a stone.' " Jesus said to him, "Again it is written, 'You shall not tempt the Lord your God.' "*—Matthew 4:5–7

I

THE PROPHET AMOS ONCE SKETCHED some hilarious cartoons about the people of Israel. He described a man running for dear life with a lion in hot pursuit, only to run into a bear; or one who barely makes it to his cabin, slams the door, slumps up against the wall—and is bitten by a serpent (5:19). That sort of reversal has always been a favorite theme for film cartoons. But it can also help us describe the relationship between the first and second temptations in Matthew's story of the three temptations; There is no sharp break between the first two temptations; they are in a way continuous. Escaping the first temptation often means running into the second; standing in the first often means falling into the second—and vice versa.

Jesus stood firmly in the first temptation by referring to something more than his hunger for bread, and to something more than his desire for self-discipline or willpower as virtues in themselves. In so doing he came to a freedom from hunger greater than that which comes with having bread or fortitude in itself. He learned something about the practice of human freedom in the world, a freedom from any exclusive attention to one's own physical hungers through pursuit of further appropriate ends. He learned to live "by *every* word as it proceeds from the mouth of God." The second temptation begins right where the first temptation left off: with Jesus' very trust in such "words of God." "Very well then," the tempter says in effect, "let's see how far you will go in trusting one of those words of God." He cites a "word of God" from the psalms and asks Jesus to go ahead and live by it.

This temptation is particularly subtle because it seems to be a very "religious" or "holy" thing that Jesus is asked to do. He is taken to the most "religious" of all places and surrounded by the "holiest" of things: he is placed in the holy city, at the very pinnacle of the holy temple, where the tempter quotes the Holy Scriptures about the holy angels. All this holiness might seem overwhelming and might even begin to take on a lure all its own. We could describe this as a temptation to *be* religious or, as we say, to be "deeply religious." The voice of temptation may speak not only out of physical desires but out of desires to be spiritual, out of a desire to be above ordinary physical necessities or to ignore them. It has often been noted that the most subtle and insidious temptations come out of what a man gratuitously calls his "higher nature." Luther observed that "it is exactly our religiousness which we like to oppose to God." Bonhoeffer warned against "trying to be more religious than God himself." In Dostoevski's story, the Grand Inquisitor spoke to Christ about a persisting appetite in human life for "mystery, miracle, and authority": "Thou didst hope that man, following thee, would cling to God and not ask for a miracle. . . . But man seeks not so much God as the miraculous."

Luther once described the regular ways in which things work in the world, the laws of nature and the institutions of family and society, as "masks of God" within which he does his work of feeding, clothing, housing, protecting, educating, and entertaining his children. Using that old phrase, we might distinguish between the first two temptations as follows: the first temptation was to seize God's "masks" (the bread, technology, business, social and political programs by which he "feeds" us), forgetting the "face of God" behind or beyond them; the second temptation is to try to seize God himself, or to deal face-to-face with God, without reference to the "masks" through which he speaks, governs, and leads in the world. The first temptation may be described as that of the "secularist" man, the second temptation as that of the "religious" man. But at bottom the temptations are the same: they are temptations to give up that humanity which comes with responding to "every word that proceeds from the mouth of God"—whether by neglecting that word or by misconstruing it. The point is not that a man is a little bit of both, partly secular and partly religious, such that each must have its due. The very use of these words in that sense, as though a man were two separate beings or belonged to two separate worlds, helps to set up this pair of seductions, or results from our having been seduced, or both.

II

The "religious temptation" begins in an especially religious place with words about some especially holy things. But the rapture is calculated to become most overpowering when the tempter appeals to his prospect's own religious convictions or spiritual ambitions: "If you are the Son of God, throw yourself down." Remember—since no Son of God would ever forget—the promises about the angels! Now if ever there was a time for a Son not to appear distrustful of God, this was it. And if ever there was a time for God to openly vindicate a Son, this would seem to be it. Yet Jesus does not call such reasoning "trusting God"; he calls it "tempting God." "Again it is written, 'You shall not tempt the Lord your God.'"

If this was more than a matching of wits to get out of a tight spot, or a matching of Bible verses to support different points of view (as religious people are known to do), then we must ask what was really at issue here. Once again, we have come up against a fundamental question of what faith is or what it means to live by faith. Jesus has said that a man is to live not by bread alone but "by every word that proceeds from the mouth of God," and this meant for him a very present proceeding of that word—just as his basic proclamation of the "kingdom of God" included an active reign or ruling by God. The very point of that ancient word from Deuteronomy was that he had to be listening for the word coming to him in his own testing in the wilderness. The tempter, however, takes off from that phrase as though it meant not "by every word *as it* proceeds from the mouth of God" but "by every word which *ever* proceeded from the mouth of God," paying no attention to the particular situation in which it was first spoken or to the particular situation in which it is spoken again. Once we have separated in this way the "words which God spoke" from the "God who is speaking," we are able to do a strange thing: we are able at will to choose an ancient word with which to turn around and try to test God.

Now it is one thing, and a very appropriate thing, for faith in every circumstance to take God at his word, in the confidence that those who trust in him will never be confounded, to "taste and see that the Lord is good." It is quite another thing to take a word once spoken, any word of our choice, and "try to see God." It is one thing to speak a word of assurance to someone who walks faithfully and obediently amid danger, for he may indeed be borne up by a confidence not derived from more ordinary sources. But it is quite another thing to speak a word of assurance to one who leaps into danger with insufficient cause or skill in order to prove something to himself; the word to him in that instance is only, "What are you doing here?" What looks like a case of extraordinary confidence turns out to be at bottom a case of lack of confidence. Quoting words to God is not identical with listening to him; putting God to the test is not identical with trusting him or learning from him. On the contrary, it creates a situation in which God is to be obedient to one's own choosing, in which his hand is to be forced. To do that, whatever the outcome, is not to conquer in this temptation of faith; it is to *have fallen already*.

The first temptation was not overcome simply by developing the virtues of self-denial or willpower; and the second is not overcome simply by concentrating on one's own confidence or lack of it. One man who knew the subtleties and perils of taking the measure or the temperature of one's own faith was Martin Luther. He saw two ways in which preoccupation with one's own religiousness may lead one to tempt God or to demand a sign, namely, when it produces complacency or despair.

Complacency is particularly a threat to "religious" people precisely because they are apt to speak of themselves as "having the word of God" or as "having the grace of God," and because they know they are supposed to be trustful in these matters. "Holy Scriptures," "holy church," "holy ministry," "sacred theology," "sacred liturgy"—these are all useful phrases insofar as they serve to remind us that we are more dealt with than dealing in all of these things, and that we are dealt with by them in ways which qualify all our other dealings. But such phrases can also be occasions for temptation if we imagine that we have the holy itself in our own hands so that we may control or dispense it or count on it to bless whatever else we take in hand. Simply to *have* the truth or to *have* the word is no longer to seek it or to ask for it; it is, rather, to lose the very possibility of being *led* by it. Simply to *know* the grace of God is no longer to *receive* it or to be shaped by it in any way. To "have" and to "know" in these ways is to lose the very thing we thought we had and knew. All we have left is our own words. If we are successful or prosperous we say, "Somebody up there likes me." If we fall victim to some unforeseen catastrophe or stupidly bungle some project we say, "Somebody up there is testing me." Never does "somebody down here" have to re-examine or alter his ways. We call it "peace of mind"; Jesus called it "tempting God."

It is possible for an entire group to put God to the test in this way. If we say, as a church or a nation, "We are children of God and no evil shall befall us," and name the evils which will never befall us for this reason, the question is whether a greater evil has not already overtaken us. If we say, "We are the church, therefore the gates of hell will not prevail against us," and mean by the "gates of hell" the people who compete with us or otherwise represent a threat to us, the question is whether those gates have not already closed behind us. If a nation imagines that its policies must prevail or that it will surely be saved from all of its troubles because it is traditionally or predominantly Christian or devoted to moral and spiritual values—that God will bear it up on his hands lest it dash its foot against a stone—what is that but an attempt to mobilize God? This is a kind of corporate, national seduction in which the religious may unwittingly help to play the tempter. Those who remember the second temptation sense a solemn foreboding in widespread social attitudes like that.

There is, on the other side of it, an inner despair which threatens the religious. They, and only they, are tempted to demand a special sign or proof or experience of God's rule or God's grace. For lack of such a sign, they grow a lump in their threats or nurse a grievance (unbelievers can be more cool). Among people who seek such signs there is likely to be more talk of grace than freedom of grace, more questioning the word than hearing it, more defending the word than being led by it, more interest in marching like a mighty army than in self-emptying with Christ.

Thus the despairing believer tries by his own efforts to create the sign which has not been given. In addition to the word and the grace he professes to believe, and really in defiance of them, he tries to make himself a pious or holy man— perhaps by performing especially religious or holy works, which are therefore likely to be bizarre. (The function of faith is simply to produce "good" works.) Once when Luther became aware of this temptation within himself, he saw a familiar grin hovering in mid-air: "Thou holy devil, thou wouldst make me a saint!" The only thing to do, he said, was to listen again to words like those of the Lord to Paul, "My grace is sufficient for you, for my power is made perfect in weakness," or to the words of the Gospel that Jesus did not come "to call the righteous, but sinners to repentance"—and to prefer to remain a sinner with Christ rather than to become a saint with the devil. Then, lest we return to romantic or sentimental dissection of our own attitudes, he advised that we do something suggested by the situation itself, something not at all "religious," such as enjoying a cooling drink, the company of a maid, or some sweaty work in the soil.

Both false security and despair take their toll in the loss of engaged activity in the world. The former makes us unresponsive to new challenges, obligations, and opportunities day by day; the latter uses up our energies in self-searching petulance and self-justifying actions. In both we have passed the place where these very attacks might have provided the occasion for a new perspective, where a stultifying inwardness might have ended with our looking outward to Christ, where the very denial of a sign might have brought a new understanding of responsibility in the world. Then, instead of asking for a sign, we might have learned to say as in a psalm: "I have laid up thy word in my heart, that I might not sin against thee" (Ps. 119:11); or with Luther: "God has taken care of my salvation; now I can take care of those things entrusted to me!"

III

We are in danger of the treachery of the second temptation each time we talk about "God" or the "word of God" and are not talking about what these imply in the world, or each time we talk about "faith" or "trust in God" without getting on with appropriate engagements. No man is properly employed when he is jumping off a temple pinnacle to test God's presence or responsiveness in the world. He *is* properly employed when he is attentive to falling bodies, seeking to describe the laws of motion, or manufacturing parachutes—and installing an auxiliary rip cord. It is when we put things to experimental test that we do *not* tempt God. It follows that if we do not wish to tempt God we must put all things to experimental test.

In Bertolt Brecht's *Galileo,* this proto-typical scientist and scholar is presented as a student of moving bodies, not as a man unusually scrupulous in his commercial dealings, nor as a devoted father, nor as a moral hero concerned with living a frugal life or dying a exemplary death. The kind of evidence Galileo offers for his scientific theorems is the kind offered by his telescope, his mathematics, and the stones he carries in his pocket. When at the climax of the play Galileo is confronted by the Inquisitor's machines, the capacities of which Galileo understands very well, he recants and is released. Returning to the street, he is met by former colleagues, whereupon the following exchange takes place.

FRIEND: Unhappy is the land that breeds no hero.
GALILEO: No, unhappy is the land that needs a hero.

Martyrdom would not prove a physical theorem. The new science would be advanced by placing one's evidence and one's formulations on the line, not one's body or head. Inquiry and evidence constituted the appropriate responsiveness, respect, and even reverence, in such matters.

If (as we saw in Jesus' reply to the first temptation) there are times and issues in which one must be willing to risk or offer his life, there are also times and issues (as we see in the second temptation) in which it is inappropriate to do so. One does not picket in behalf of the law of gravity. Where more public, objective, communicable, and cumulative evidence must be decisive, there are regular techniques for keeping one's "self" or one's more personal viewpoints out of one's calculations and arguments. A good course in logic, or even a computer, may provide a precaution against abuse in such matters. When one is tempted to make a personal or religious issue out of a scientific argument, the reply to that temptation must be, "My hour has not yet come." Resisting such temptations might help prepare one to say at the right time and on the right issue, "The hour has come."

A similar failure to seek God in his "masks" occurs each time we speak of God's "providence" or "protection" without any reference to the supermarket on the corner or the policeman on the beat, or when we include these in our prayers without at the same time inquiring what must be done to facilitate or improve such services, or when the clergyman is left to do such praying on our behalf. There is no surer way of separating our work from our praying, as well as from any neglected demands or joys which might be revealed in prayer. Think of the dinners to which clergymen have been invited, for which the man of the house has labored through the week and for which the woman of the house has spent the day in the kitchen. Yet when the great moment arrives it is the holy man who is asked to thank God for the gifts of the table (you should have tasted them when God had them alone). Would it not be more appropriate, and in a way more faithful, for that man to thank his hosts for inviting him and perhaps also thank God for his hosts—and leave *them* to thank God for the dinner as they will?

When we move from the "masks" of the sciences and services to those of political programs which make provisions for public activities, the possibilities of tempting God become more subtle. If, for example, we oppose public welfare in the name of private charity, is it because we are more interested in a special sign or exercise of our own goodness than we are concerned that all the hungry should be fed and all citizens should have an adequate roof overhead? If we support public programs for the poor but oppose organization and movement among the poor, is it because we are thinking of an orderly, respectable, virtuous, or fiscally attractive society rather than of a politically active one? ("We don't want our city to get a bad reputation" calls forth many a grin in the ghetto.) Do we not occasionally lament the fact that our private and public generosity receives few confirming responses from the recipients? "We gave them all that welfare and we got Watts!" "We gave them a new high school and still they drop out!" "They all have TV's and still they're restless!"

Our virtues, even unthanked ones, are not the entire issue. Building a good society in which all are able to participate and reshaping institutions so that a variety of participating interests can be represented are projects which are no less important than those of pursuing physics or profit or charitable projects. All men are responsible for success or failure in such tasks. President John F. Kennedy was thinking about the importance of political activity for all other activities when he reminded us at the close of his inaugural address that "God's work must truly be our own."

Similar questions might be asked of "purer" but feebler actions for social reform. We are all familiar with the "lonely witness," one man or a tiny group standing alone for a social belief and being ignored, jeered, or even attacked for that stand. This seems in some ways admirable, and it might even be appropriate if there is no hope of achieving any practical discussion or action. But is not the second temptation close by, that of the solitary, righteous action taken before God without thought of the ways of working effectively in the world of men? Of being willing to die for a good cause but not to work for it? Appropriate social action is taken through discussion and organization. Pursuing that course bespeaks hope and expectancy with respect to one's fellow men, as well as modesty with respect to one's own opinions. It is no mark of human dignity to march with a peashooter against a tank. The work of organization is no less perilous, certainly no less arduous, than that of lonely witness. It seems a likely intention, in political matters, to resolve to go down organizing if one must go down at all. Even in that event one would not merely question the good will or good faith of other men. He would have reason to question his own judgment, effort, or skill.

IV

The tempter of this gospel story is out to seduce the religious, not to put an end to religion. Many in the last century who have seen how seductive religion can become, and the trouble it can then cause in such activities as the development of physical theory, the practice of psychotherapy, or the work of societal reform, have spoken of an end to religion and have even welcomed it. Yet an utter disregard for the freedom, vision, and celebration of faith might, as we have seen, put us back into the jaws of the first temptation.

For wisdom in this matter may we not apply to the victor in these temptations? Day after day, as the Gospels tell it, He is followed by religious people who seek to catch him in a fault, a sign-in-reverse which might discredit the demand he makes on human life. When they seek, incongruously, a "sign from heaven" to verify his conception of faith, Jesus speaks some harsh words: "An evil and adulterous generation seeks for a sign." He adds something which should strike a familiar chord in us: "But no sign shall be given to it except the sign of the prophet Jonah." Jonah was denied the particular sign he sought but was given a quite different sign in the waters. "For as Jonah was three days and three nights in the belly of the whale, so will the Son of man be three days and nights in the heart of the earth." This amounted to a reversal of what Jesus' pursuers had asked. The Son of Man would go, as the very sign of his authenticity, to a faithful death without vindication in the eyes of his gainsayers. Nineveh, for all its pagan simplicity, had responded to the call of the hour more directly than those who now sought a sign: "The men of Nineveh will arise at the judgment with this generation and condemn it; for they repented at the preaching of Jonah, and behold, something greater than Jonah is here" (Matt. 12:38-42).

When it comes to his passion, Jesus is prosecuted by religious as well as political leaders, and perhaps more for religious than political reasons. "He who delivered me to you has the greater sin," Jesus says to the worldly politician Pontius Pilate in the Fourth Gospel (John 19:11). The most bitter words beneath the cross are spoken by religious men who are still calling for a sign from heaven to show the validity of Jesus' faith—a faith for which, even then and there, no such sign would be given. "He trusts in God; let God deliver him now, if he desires him; for he said, 'I am the Son of God.' " When Jesus cries from the psalms out of the temptation of the cross, "Eli, Eli, lama sabachthani?" ("My God, my God, why has thou forsaken me?"), the religious make a pun, saying he was calling for Elijah. "Wait, let us see whether Elijah will come to save him" (Matt. 27:43-49). In the Gospel of Mark, the passersby throw back at Jesus his nettling words about the temple: "You who would destroy the temple and build it in three days, save yourself, and come down from the cross!" The chief priests and scribes also take up this chant: "He saved others; he cannot save himself. Let the Christ, the King of Israel, come down now from the cross, that we may see and believe" (Mark 15:29-32). Did they not see that if he was to save *others* he could not save himself? That the God of his faith was being faithful to the world in this Son, to the very men who moped and boasted, slept and fled, mocked and quoted Bible texts in order to escape such faithfulness? If Jesus *had* stepped down from the cross, *what* would they have to believe?

Where can the man of faith be found today? To be sure, he is reading the Scriptures to see how the word came to expression in times and places past—but not simply to repeat favorite words in the face of new situations. The very point of those words was that a man should be similarly responsive in every new, unprecedented situation. Accordingly, the faithful man can also be found in the laboratory, watching and listening to actual processes in the world; he is conducting surveys in order to understand how the people themselves define their needs and regard the workings of society; he is engaged in political processes by which institutions are directed to appropriately chosen ends. He is to be found, moreover, in unaccustomed places. He knows there are obligations to be met that the law, which deals only in present equities, does not itself require—the special needs which people have because they are different from one another, and the additional tasks to be assumed because of inequities long borne in the very blood and bones of the society or because of new opportunities present within it. He takes up such tasks for others, sustaining a hope for them even though they ignore such burdens. He does all this not as any extraordinary or "religious" service but because it is needed, because this is how one responds as a man. He is completing what remains of Christ's afflictions (Col. 1:24). Anything less would amount to "tempting God." So would any lack of candor about the prudential judgments he has made.

If such watchfulness and activity do not in fact characterize the religious today, if they seem "out of it," if they appear less responsive than others to new projects imposed by a changing society or appear willing to leave them to others, if they *do* seem to be tempting God—what are we to make of that? Is it because the salt has lost its savor, in which case, as Jesus said, it might as well be cast out? Has this "salt" become lost from the world just when it is needed most? Or has that function passed on to others who are closer to the struggle? Have both God and the devil taken their business elsewhere? Are the religious abandoned to something far, far worse than the wilderness or the cross—to a land of dreams in which they are no longer tempted at all?

SEVEN

Beyond Seduction

Again, the devil took him to a very high mountain, and showed him all the kingdoms of the world and the glory of them; and he said to him, "All these I will give you, if you will fall down and worship me." Then Jesus said to him, "Begone, Satan! for it is written, 'You shall worship the Lord your God and him only shall you serve.'" Then the devil left him, and behold, angels came and ministered to him.—Matthew 4:8–11

I

"OH, TO GET ONE'S TEETH into a Herod again, or a Henry the Eighth, or even a Hitler!" So wrote the devil Screwtape in a letter discovered too late to be included in *The Screwtape Letters* but subsequently published in *The Saturday Evening Post.* Today's sinners, he complained, are "hardly, if at all, in a state of full spiritual responsibility. . . . Their consciousness hardly exists apart from the social atmosphere that surrounds them. And, of course, we have contrived that their language should be all smudge and blur." What this devil seems to be saying is that men and women are so easily taken in by the first and second temptations that they hardly ever get on to the third. With most people, there is no need to bring out the third temptation; they are already in the bag. The devil has many dupes in the world but very few honest-to-goodness (or honest-to-badness) disciples.

In order to face the most fundamental issues in human life, our text is saying, we must pass through the first two temptations to the third. Jesus passed through the first two temptations, which spoke respectively out of "physical" and "spiritual" desires that seemed legitimate enough when verbally separated. He was upheld in both by a word of God, by what he saw as a demand upon him and other men which did not come simply from his own physical hunger or spiritual thirst. So—but only so—Jesus becomes a candidate for the last temptation. There is no longer any question of deceiving Jesus into a loss of genuine faith or of a corresponding manhood. Accordingly, the tempter comes to him without any dissimulation—and, it seems, with a certain degree of respect.

On this occasion the devil does not begin by saying, "If you are the Son of God. . . ." He does not quote the Scriptures. The approach is more like one that begins, "Now, you're the kind of man I can admire"; or, "You're not the kind of man to toy with"; or, "You're the kind of man who likes to see things the way they are—very well, then, how *are* things in the world?" or, "Let's level with each other." The devil shows Jesus a kind of power which can be achieved in the world and which actually gets response and gets things done. "All this will I give you. . . ."

It won't do to say that the tempter is being deceitful because he has nothing of the sort to offer, because the power and the glory of the world aren't his to give. He is talking about what actually works, and actually pays, in visible and tangible ways. In one sense, he is talking about how to succeed in such a way as *not* to be deceived. What "succeeds" in the world is not necessarily "good" in moral terms and what is "good" does not necessarily "succeed" in ordinary terms. A certain kind of power and glory *can* come to one who takes things the way they are, who gives people what they want and what they are willing to pay well for with no further questions asked. The New Testament is candid in calling the devil the "prince of this world." For his part, Jesus does not dispute the plausibility of the offer. This is a genuine temptation for Jesus only if he is realistic enough to know that there is this kind of power and glory in the world, and confident enough to know that he could have his share of it.

Neither will it do to say that this temptation is not real because, after all, God could and would in some continuous sense top the offer. Jesus knows, after the first and second temptations, what God actually offers a loyal Son in the world; he has already felt something of the pain, the weakness, and the loneliness of obedience. At bottom the question is this: Does he want power and glory in the ways these are actually offered and recognized in the world, or does he want more waiting, more weariness, more suffering? Does he choose— the cross? The devil wants Jesus to make the choice in full view of all the realities of the situation—and he wants to hear him make it!

In one sense, it is a mark of distinction to qualify for the third temptation. Only those who have seen the seductions of the first two temptations, and have seen through them, ever really encounter the third. This is the most conscious of the temptations; one might even define the third temptation as fully-conscious temptation. It comes only to one who is no longer deceiving himself about the world in order to shield himself. It is a temptation which comes to knaves but never to fools. There is a certain value simply in being awake to it. There is an undeniable, even enviable, candor in the question Jean Shepherd asks on behalf of all of us: "Where do you line up to sell out?"

The third temptation comes *only* to those who have been through the first and second temptations, and it comes *inevitably* to them. The first two temptations, once their implications are clearly seen, become the third. Very well, since you can't be seduced, what do you *choose*? People who belong to the seducer anyway can always wake up to what they're doing and join up with him. Certainly that choice confronts all who have allowed this story to open their eyes.

Can we see the sense in which this is the "last" temptation? There is no longer any question of deception. The issues are entirely clear. One who has fallen heedlessly into the trap of the first or second temptation has yet to see the third; but one whose eyes are opened to the third temptation has reached a point of no return. If he falls in the last temptation, no further temptation is necessary. If he stands firm in the face of the last temptation, no further temptation is possible.

II

The third temptation introduces a new complexity: its focus is not simply on what we think about ourselves or wish for ourselves, but on what we think about and seek for other people. We are now looking not at our own flesh or our own spirit but at "all the kingdoms of the world and the glory of them." "We are not contending against flesh and blood, but against the principalities, against the powers, against the world rulers of this present darkness" (Eph. 6:12). Would Jesus, who had resisted within himself any overruling demand for bread, seek nothing less in the people he served? Would he refuse a kingship which could be acquired by catering to the people's clamor for bread—even if sharp controversy resulted and many no longer walked with him? Would he who had resisted within himself a desire to manipulate God and holy things also refuse when others implored him to do so for the sake of the people? Would he refuse to make use of their religious beliefs and superstitions in attaching them to himself—even if it meant losing the people to other leaders and suffering their bitter rejections? What kind of public good could he possibly do after that?

People who (as the Grand Inquisitor described them) are disposed to cry, "Make us your slaves but feed us," are an easy prey for the first temptation. Those who look for "mystery, miracle, and authority," who "love not so much God as the miraculous," fall easily to the second temptation. Only the Grand Inquisitor himself, who sees all these things clearly and speaks of them lucidly, really confronts the issue of the third temptation. After fifteen hundred years it has become clear, he says, that Jesus made the wrong decision in the wilderness. The people would never take up life on such high terms but they would give their loyalty to anyone who made them comfortable on simpler terms. The Inquisitor makes his choice consciously, even sorrowfully, for the sake of people who do not really want to make any hard choices at all. "It is expedient," every Caiaphas has always said, ". . . for the people."

The third temptation comes on the scene, then, with considerations like these: "Since people are the way they are"; "The world being the way it is"; "One has to begin with people where they are"; "Think of how many more we might help if"; "There is no use in disturbing the people"; "What can you do if you don't have the people with you?" One who yields to this temptation does so with responses like these: "If I had only myself to think about, but"; "If we had only ourselves to think about, but"; "It's not my world, I didn't make it"; "If I don't, somebody else will." Sentences which begin in these ways may, and usually do, refer to factual and relevant considerations. But they may also represent a capitulation to the last temptation, in which one agrees to let the world go to the devil and makes the most of it on such terms, in which one allows the standard seductions to prevail and perhaps even profits as a seducer, in which one does nothing to keep people from living in smaller houses than that opened by faith and even shacks up with them there.

One of the most memorable scenes in the modern theater is Peter Weiss's dramatic portrayal of Jean-Paul Marat, firebrand of the French Revolution, seated in his bathtub four years after the fall of the Bastille treating a rare and fitful skin disease, but still calling for pen and ink to write his "July 13 call to the people of France." He is assassinated in his tub by a beautiful former colleague, Charlotte Corday, who sides now with patrician order against continued bloodshed. Meanwhile the chorus fights over bottles, falls asleep, and chants popular ditties such as:

> Marat we're poor and the poor stay poor
> Marat don't make us wait any more
> We want our rights and we don't care how
> We want our revolution NOW

and,

> What's the point of revolution
> without general copulation

and at the very end, with Marat dead,

> Marat we're marching on behind Napoleon.

No wonder the brilliant revolutionary has a rash. No wonder the Marquis de Sade, once a supporter of the revolution, now commends and cultivates private sentience over mass sentiments in the face of a detestably silent nature. The argument is dramatically complicated in the play, but all are made to feel the age-old split between what the individual desires and what can be achieved in the mass.

Does not the need to maintain civic order, and accordingly to exercise power in society, necessarily precede the development of democratic institutions, which take a long time to develop? The most popular movements require strong, charismatic leaders and make their appeal to bread-and-butter issues. Even the civil rights movement was led in many of its first engagements by clergymen and focused on the people's most fundamental needs. When deprived communities organize in the big cities, rarely more than 4 per cent of the people become politically active. Even for that the issues must be simplified; "self-interest" is often the explicit cry. There is little room, at least at first, for any dissident minority; dissenters are likely to become a target of mobilizing activity. Even the most "democratic" movements call upon leaders who will exert a certain coercive influence, accept a certain "glory," think in terms of numbers, and raise the kinds of issues which will get the most response. Otherwise, there is likely to be no "organization" or "movement" at all.

Such facts seem sufficient to raise the question of the political-ecclesiastical Inquisitor afresh. After four hundred more years, what would we say? Does anyone seriously believe that the multitudes can become interested in a sustained way in something more than bread—and other products? Isn't it necessary to be product-oriented for the sake of the economy? Can people really become political activists at a time when things are changing so rapidly, on so large a scale, and in such interdependent ways, as to make popular judgments difficult? How can they do so while the media themselves are devoted to selling bread rather than to discussing issues, and while they sell more bread with Westerns than with "East Side, West Side," or with secret agents than with "The Defenders." In such a climate—in which politics itself tends to become show-biz—who can really eschew the ordinary ways to power and glory?

Is even the church going to resist these? Do not churches themselves seek the usual kind of influence and prestige—a public image acceptable to the most people? Don't they adapt their message to the predilections of the rich among the rich, as well as to those of the poor among the poor, in order to secure a following in both groups—preaching a mesage of comfort to people for whom having or coveting comforts is already a way of life? Don't they have to be "interested in numbers"? What if they weren't? Doesn't Jesus' answer to the third temptation really amount to a withdrawal from life as it is, and actually lend itself to reaction? Wasn't the Grand Inquisitor right after all—for the sake of the people?

What *would* it mean to follow Christ in resisting. this temptation today? The answer, insofar as it refers to actions taken in the public realm, is not a simple one. Following Christ need not mean forswearing every use of power or influence, for that would leave decisions affecting us all to those who do choose to use power or influence, and also limit their ability to adopt what we would regard as enlightened policies. Power is a created good, and it is there to be used wisely and enjoyed. But following Christ *would* mean confirming power wherever it has been *created,* not merely wherever it has been *accumulated.* That means confirming power within every man, who must learn to appreciate and use his own power both singly and in association with others. Accordingly, it would mean rejecting any final validity in the concept of the masses or any merely venal use of the media. It would mean choosing the way of confrontation, contention, deliberation, decision, and delegation of powers for specified ends—over the offers of titans, fuehrers, duces, high priests, and bosses who know what's good for the people and are doing everything for their good (and who, if you object to their approach, are likely to know what's good for you). It would mean accepting the task to educate as well as to lead, even though alternative solutions to public problems are much harder to dispense than bread. It would mean valuing the political practice above the public image, though both the powerful and the powerless may be only too willing to accept the image and forsake the practice. It would mean choosing a continuous exercise of that practice over any single great crusade, any single choice of policy, or any particular movement which offers to "give us evermore this bread." It would mean refusing to confer or to accept the power and the glory which often await one who offers the quick, easy, or final solution—though by this indispensable refusal one makes himself as dispensable as any other man. One who resists the third temptation with Christ is no longer given to making every accommodation because he thinks everybody needs him. That amounts to a denial of what everybody really needs. What everybody needs most is space in which to act with relative safety and freedom as a human agent. Free decisions and actions cannot, of course, be legislated, but conditions conducive to such actions can be. To insist on opening such spaces throughout the society, and to work at keeping them open, is still to take up a cross in hope.

For those who work with this intent, the question is sure to recur: How did it really come out in the wilderness? Who was the winner after all? Jesus walked off the field to a cross. The tempter has enjoyed many a field day since. Was the victory perhaps only a Pyrrhic victory, too small a victory at too great a cost? Or a draw? There is no decisive evidence or argument to support us in moments of the third temptation. Much reasoning and much plain evidence take part in the attack against us. Even sentiment and compassion may fall on the side of the temptation rather than on the side of victory in that temptation. They may serve as weapons in the hand of the tempter; they cannot always be used decisively against him. Only one reply will serve to withstand this temptation, a reply which does not come simply from our own insides or from the opinion polls but through Him who in this lesson conquered. It does not mince: "Begone, Satan! for it is written, 'You shall worship the Lord your God and him only shall you serve.'"

The devil may cut a romantic figure in our imaginations (as in *Faust* or *Paradise Lost*), but we are not in the light of this lesson to play with the devil or to try our dialectical skill with him. (Remember Eve?) Having a dialogue with the devil could mean the end of every dialogue with men and the beginning of public speeches. We are often disposed to romanticize our religious tussles, our difficulties in matters of faith, our confusions about "God," and no doubt these are all serious enough. But we are not, in the light of this lesson, to put them on stage. All the world's a stage, and the question is who or what *are* we going to worship and serve—even *while* we examine our doubts.

III

"Then the devil left him, and behold, angels came and ministered to him." Our story ends, as it began, with strange words. A certain peace has come onto the scene, but it is not a peace which is familiar from ordinary usage. It is not a peace which comes in obvious ways: by eating after prolonged hunger, or by receiving a delayed approval or recognition. It is a peace which can be present in the absence of bread or applause—or in the midst of them—but which is therefore not to be identified with them. It is not a listless or lethargic peace, one which comes in the absence of strife or by not seeing any strife. It comes to one who sees a pain and a terror, as well as a mystery and a majesty, which he did not see so clearly before. In short, this is not the kind of peace which one chooses and then achieves for himself. It is from the start, and remains at the end, a gift. That is how the Fourth Gospel describes the peace of Christ: "Peace I leave with you; my peace I give to you; not as the world gives do I give to you" (John 14:27).

In the story of Gethsemane, where Jesus watched and waited, we read again that "an angel came from heaven strengthening him." In the scenes that follow, those who slept in the garden will be frantic, while He who stayed awake will be at peace. He will stand calmly while his disciples fall over one another trying to be the first to get away and while his captors stumble over one another trying to stay in the back row. He will be firm before a fumbling Sanhedrin, composed before a powerful Pilate, silent before an inquisitive Herod. He will pray for the soldiers who drive nails through his hands. He will provide for his mother and counsel a thief from the cross. In all these frenzied scenes, Jesus will be at peace: he will be at the heart of every struggle, and yet free within each struggle. There is a certain kingship and glory in Jesus after all—above that of "all the kingdoms of the world and the glory of them," and yet within them.

"You are those who have continued with me in my trials," Jesus says to his disciples near the close of Luke's Gospel. "As my Father appointed a kingdom for me, so do I appoint for you" (Luke 22:28 f.). Everything depends on continuing in his temptations, on seeing and meeting life's occasions with Christ. The focus must never be merely on *our* struggles or *our* ideals. The crying of our flesh and the bleating of our spirit may often have the first word but never the last. When we continue in *his* temptations, it is not our religion or lack of religion which occupy us, but his obedient faith. It is not our doubts that most occupy us but his steadfastness. If we are tempted with him, we triumph with him. If we suffer with him, we reign with him. We are given a kingdom which comes by no institutional appointment—and the glory of it. "Now is the Son of man glorified," Jesus says in the Fourth Gospel when he turns to face his death, and he prays that the same glory may be given to his disciples (John 13:31; 17:22).

To "see" this is to see all problems in a new light, whether they be matters of bread, religion, or politics. It is to view all engagements with other men and women in a new light, and this may help to fashion a special style of meeting, discoursing, working, and celebrating with them. But this "seeing" is not something that any man can simply give to another. It requires, in fact, that we keep our hands off one another and make room for one another in hope. Together with all the other things we owe each other, we always at the same time owe one another a wish, a prayer, and occasionally even a word like this: "The peace of God, which passes all understanding, keep your hearts and your minds in Christ Jesus" (Phil. 4:7).

Holy Week:

Of Wakings

EIGHT

A Cup for All Occasions

*The cup of blessing which we bless, is it not a participation in the
blood of Christ? The bread which we break, is it not a participation
in the body of Christ? . . . So, whether you eat or drink, or whatever you do, do all to the glory of God.*

—I Corinthians 10:16, 31

*But in the following instructions I do not commend you, because
when you come together it is not for the better but for the worse.
For, in the first place, when you assemble as a church, I hear that
there are divisions among you; and I partly believe it, for there
must be factions among you in order that those who are genuine
among you may be recognized. When you meet together, it is not
the Lord's supper that you eat. For in eating, each one goes ahead
with his own meal, and one is hungry and another is drunk. What!
Do you not have houses to eat and drink in? Or do you despise the
church of God and humiliate those who have nothing? What shall
I say to you? Shall I commend you in this? No, I will not.*

*For I received from the Lord what I also delivered to you, that
the Lord Jesus on the night when he was betrayed took bread,
and when he had given thanks, he broke it, and said, "This is my
body which is for you. Do this in remembrance of me." In the
same way also the cup, after supper, saying, "This cup is the new
covenant in my blood. Do this, as often as you drink it, in remembrance of me." For as often as you eat this bread and drink the
cup, you proclaim the Lord's death until he comes.*

*Whoever, therefore, eats the bread or drinks the cup of the Lord
in an unworthy manner will be guilty of profaning the body and
blood of the Lord. Let a man examine himself, and so eat of the
bread and drink of the cup. For any one who eats and drinks
without discerning the body eats and drinks judgment upon himself.
That is why many of you are weak and ill, and some have died.*

—I Corinthians 11:17–30

101

He took the cup. . . .—I Corinthians 11:25 (K.J.V.)

It is truly meet, right, and salutary, that we should at all times, and in all places, give thanks. . . .—Preface, The Holy Communion

WE HAVE SPOKEN ABOUT VARIETIES of "sleep" which may come over us all. In every case, eyes were closed or wits were dulled to something which was in some way there waiting to be recognized—so it always appeared to those who came "awake" and talked about it. We wish to devote our last three reflections to the kinds of jolts which may serve to wake us up, which may open our eyes to see what faith claims to see.

Such awakenings may take place, according to the texts we shall consider, when and where we least expect them or in connection with the most familiar things. The various elements of the scenes described are familiar enough, or were familiar to those who first described them, and yet there is a strange juxtaposition which makes us begin to stir. A celebration takes place on the occasion of a death; a royal procession leads directly to a humiliating, yet still somehow kingly, execution; a sad gathering in old haunts becomes the occasion for joyful discernment and a new commission scattering the gatherers in every direction. The differing parts of these pictures seem strangely joined; one stretches, squirms—and wakes up to see that they might really belong together!

Participants in the Lord's Supper remember a man's death and share bread and wine together. These actions are in themselves familiar, and yet when taken together they make a disturbing combination—or did for the people who first remembered and broke bread together. On just such an occasion, according to the gospel, "their eyes were opened."

I

It is of utmost importance to remember that in the stories of the Gospels the Supper which Jesus kept with his disciples was held "on the night when he was betrayed." All the Gospels take pains to point this out; all weave words about the betrayal into the story of the Supper, and all show that Jesus was already aware of the betrayal at the time of the Supper. The very evening on which he was to be betrayed, abandoned, and denied by those who had been closest to him, on which he would say to those who came to take him away, "This is your hour, and the power of darkness"—*that* was the occasion on which he kept the feast with his disciples.

It is equally important to remember the festal quality of this Supper. If it was the Passover, as the first three Gospels say, its purpose was to celebrate an event held by faith to be a source of constant renewal and promise, Israel's liberation from bondage in Egypt. Moreover, the Passover meal had come to be viewed as a feast of anticipation. It seems likely, from recent descriptions of the Essenes and the Qumran community in the "Dead Sea Scrolls," that this anticipation also characterized many Sabbath-eve meals, and even the daily evening meal in many families. There was the vacant chair, and the extra cup of wine, set and waiting for the Messiah should he come at the time of the meal. These were apocalyptic, celebrational banquets observed partly in anticipation of the Messiah.

The stories of the Last Supper in the first three Gospels are surrounded with this suggestion. Jesus says in a number of ways, "The hour is at hand." He alludes to the culminating feast (as many parables had referred to a "great feast"): "I have earnestly desired to eat this passover with you before I suffer; for I tell you I shall not eat it until it is fulfilled in the kingdom of God. . . . For I tell you that from now on I shall not drink of the fruit of the vine until the kingdom of God comes" (Luke 22:15 f., 18). When, later, he "takes the cup," a dramatic thought arises. Was the cup set for him by the disciples just any cup? Or was it *the* cup, the cup set for the Coming One—as if to say, "This is it; the bridegroom has come; the feast has begun!" A cup to victory with the victor and to the kingdom which he will establish! In any case, we are allowed to see that image behind this scene; and the early faithful came to see the Lord's Supper in this light.

The Supper we ourselves keep is meant to be viewed not only as a memorial of Jesus' death but as a present celebration and an anticipatory feast. The invitation at the outset is *Sursum Corda,* "Lift up your hearts." The song which follows joins Isaiah's ancient vision of the heavenly celebration to this simple feast on earth: "Holy, holy, holy . . . heaven and earth are full of thy glory." We explicitly remember the night on which Jesus was betrayed, together with the persisting cruelty of the world and the continuing betrayals and obtuseness of those who should know better. But to that narrative is added a word filled with life and light out of the Gospel stories of the Resurrection: "The peace of the Lord be with you always!" This very conjunction of death and celebration produces the peace and illumination of the *Nunc Dimittis* at the end: "Lord, now lettest thou thy servant depart in peace . . . for mine eyes have seen thy salvation . . . a light to lighten the Gentiles: and the glory of thy people Israel."

The first Supper was a strange time for a celebration, contrary to prevailing expectations concerning the kingly feast. The eyes of the disciples were not fully open either to the darkness or the light of that occasion—as the stories show with an almost salacious taste for detail. The disciples quarrel over who will be nearest the throne in the splendor of the kingdom when it comes. They boast of the heroic exploits they will perform on the way to the enthronement and count their pitiful swords. Later, while Jesus prays and sweats in the very middle of a battle they do not comprehend, they are "sleeping for sorrow." Betrayal, flight, and denial follow as a matter of course. They were not thinking of this death as the decisive witness to the kingdom; they were not ready for this celebration. We are meant to see ourselves in these pictures of the huddling, whispering, boasting, bleating disciples. We may bring little more perception or gladness to the Supper than they did. Perhaps we come to escape the realities of life. Or if we have faced those realities, perhaps we wonder why we come at all.

Why this cup on such an ordinary occasion? Why this song in an hour of social unrest and danger? In a time of rapid change on every side, producing uncertainty and demanding austerity, how can we turn to celebration—indeed, to *the* celebration, one in which we refer to a "last" or culminating celebration? Something is waiting to be discovered. In this bread and wine there are depths and heights of which we have not dreamed, to which we might awaken. "On the same night in which he was betrayed . . . he took the cup."

II

How are we to understand this death and celebration together? There is little difficulty in seeing the Lord's Supper as an occasion for remembering Jesus' *death*. The words say as much: "Do this in remembrance of me." This is, in fact, a unique, picturesque way of remembering: we break the bread and remember the body that was broken; we pour the cup and remember the blood that was shed. The bread and wine serve as visual aids; they make for a dramatic re-presentation of that death. Martin Luther called the broken bread and the poured-out wine a "visible word."

This "visible word" is unusually suited, moreover, to audience participation. It makes possible an action in response: "Take, eat"; "Take, drink." We can come forward and take it, or we can sit back and let it pass us by. That might even become part of the dramatic reenactment: some people participated more actively in Jesus' death while others were unwitting bystanders who participated nonetheless, undiscerningly, in the crucifixion. All this is plain enough and yet it is not at all clear from what we have said exactly *why* we should remember this death, or exactly what there is to *celebrate* about

105

it. On the contrary, it seems a depressing reminder of something that happens only too often in the world—with some of us helping to inflict the world's cruelties while others stand idly by. What is there to remember about that? What is there to *celebrate?*

A traditional answer, one which refers to Jesus' words in the Gospel of Matthew, is that the Supper imparts "the remission of sins." But what does that mean, and how does the Supper do so? Forgiveness is familiar as an act which passes between persons. On the basis of this interpersonal experience, one might try to conceive of God's forgiving someone his sin or of letting oneself be forgiven by God. But what does it mean that Jesus' blood should be "poured out for many for the forgiveness of sins"? What is the connection between this *death* and "sin" or between this death and "forgiveness"? And why the general *celebration?* Isn't forgiveness usually a more private affair?

For many, the Lord's Supper is primarily a communal event, a meal of fellowship. In the Fourth Gospel, Jesus says on the evening of the Supper, "A new commandment I give to you, that you love one another" (John 13:34). Eating together at a single table does serve to suggest a united family, people at peace with one another. Paul spoke not only about a single table but about a single loaf of bread: "Because there is one loaf, we who are many are one body, for we all partake of the same loaf" (I Cor. 10:17). Many feel a need for closer or more intimate personal relationships and no doubt this Supper (like other kinds of family suppers) can help to meet that need. But surely the death of Jesus is not needed to bring us together, if that is what we wish. What is the connection between our mutuality and Jesus' death? And how do our gatherings become *celebrations* by virtue of that death? Memorial, forgiveness, and fellowship are all somehow present, but they are still waiting to be illumined by that death and turned into something to celebrate.

Let us return with our questions to the Supper itself. When Paul wrote to the people in Corinth who were in danger of

losing the meaning of the Lord's Supper, he began by pointing to the bread and wine themselves, and what the participants
did with these things: "The cup of blessing which we bless,
is it not a participation in the blood of Christ? The bread
which we break, is it not a participation in the body of Christ?"
The people were to see themselves as "participants" in the
death of Jesus: to be sure, as people who "participated" by
crucifying his kind of life in one way or another, but also as
"participants" in another sense—as people who actually offered
their bodies and lives as he did. Why should they do that?
Because there was in that offered body and life something
which began to make sense both of the life which was offered
and of the world in which it was offered. Eyes are "opened"
when the death of Jesus and all other things come together
in the same picture, when the world is seen as upheld, sustained, and filled with hope by his bodily offering. Participation
in the body and blood of Christ are now seen as actions on
which other things depend and as the very way of life for men
—as "true body and blood." So we bless that cup and drink
it as a gift to us and a pledge by us in one and the same draft.
When we see this death as the paradigmatic affirmation of
life, and begin to see all of life in the light of this death, death
and celebration have come together.

Our other understandings of the Supper now return, and
they do so with surprising new force. We begin to recover
the secret of the "forgiveness of sins" when we mean by "sins"
every rejection on our part of that offered life in our world,
and when we include in "forgiveness" our own dying to
former ways and taking up this new one. We begin to recover
the secret of this "fellowship" when we no longer merely
cling to or indulge one another but stand together for a
moment in the light of this joyful demand upon us all. We
keep the feast not merely because we are touched by this
memory or wish forgiveness or choose to be together, but
because this is the way it is, the way of life which knows how
to affirm the present and which belongs to its future. We are
celebrating and appropriating a right kind of action in the

world. "It is truly meet, right, and salutary that we should. . . ."

This objective, giving-and-demanding character of the Supper is what Paul pressed on the congregation in Corinth. "I delivered to you what I also *received*. . . ." It was precisely this which was being forgotten in Corinth; people were turning the Lord's Supper back into a Supper of their own conceiving and making. At the very point of the celebration, people were asserting themselves in terms of old habits and preferences: they were segregating themselves according to old choices or accustomed classes, and "one was hungry and another was drunk." Such facts were intolerable wherever they appeared, but if they were accepted at the Supper they foreclosed the very source of help and healing. The participants were forgetting that the Lord's Supper first took place "on the night when he was betrayed." They were making their own attack on the Lord's body, no less an attack than that of those who had put Jesus to the cross; and they were doing so for the same reason—they did not discern the Lord's body. Instead of being brought to a new mode of life and a new vision of the future, they were being carried along by the most ordinary forces to the most ordinary end; some were weak, others had already died. They had forgotten the very import of the death they were remembering and therefore they had lost the celebration. If *that* was the kind of eating and drinking they wished to do, Paul said bluntly, they should do their eating and drinking at home.

It is sometimes asked whether there should be public worship at all anymore and, more specifically, whether there will always be these congregations on the corner. Paul did not directly address himself to that question. But he did say that *if* there is to be public worship, to which all are invited and which is open to the view of all men, the congregations must represent the new community of God's making and not merely some limited group of men's choosing. In the city today, a new kind of community is of necessity being formed, a community including a consciously powerful black minority. There is great reluctance to accept this fact, even greater than that which reacted to previous goals of assimilation or integration.

It will, perhaps, be generations before identity and inter-action are achieved, if that much time is given. But must not a hope be held high for the city in gatherings of faithful people who remember and celebrate the Lord's death? Might they not gather around their table, in occasional feasts of anticipation, the new family of all nations and kindreds— pointing the way to healing, wholeness, and peace against the forces of doom, sickness, and death? This is a demand and discipline of the Supper, overruling misgivings as strong in those who have been excluded as in those who have been the excluders in the past. But if a congregation is needlessly and impenitently segregated, if it *merely* perpetuates divisions in the world, has it not forgotten the death it was to remember and lost the celebration? Should it not, by all that is holy in the Holy Communion, close its doors and let its people do their eating and drinking at home?

III

It is essential that the death of Jesus always be remembered with celebration. It is equally important that celebrations should always be held with some memory of his death. It is possible to be malevolent, forgetful, or sentimental in our pleasures— in a world already sufficiently saturated with such qualities. On one occasion at Auschwitz, victims were unloaded from a box-car to strains of a Strauss waltz being played in a concert shell. That was an extreme instance of the use of entertain-ment for enforcement of interracial misconceptions and hatred, though even milder instances help to make the world a ghetto, and possibly a death camp, for us all. There are performances and pleasures which demean the personality of women, thereby undercutting the very quality of human sexual enjoyment. Other entertainments are gotten up explicitly for the sake of forgetting what is going on, for escape, or for getting away from it all for a night or a season. Sometimes the pleasure is simply sentimental and to enjoy it we have to pretend that we or the world are different than we really are. Such "happy" occasions may invoke even greater horrors than those they seek to escape, as in the celebrations depicted in unsentimental entertainments like Garcia Lorca's *Blood Wedding* or Harold Pinter's *Birthday Party*.

This is not to say that celebrations should cease until we have a better world. There is, to be sure, the civil rights leader who shaves his head, and the black child who is told not to laugh (at least not in the presence of a white man) until the present troubles are past. None of this is hard to understand and much of it may be tactically valid. And yet there is this command to celebrate: "Do this in remembrance of me." We are bidden to break the bread and bless the cup not because we wish to celebrate, or deserve to celebrate, but because there *is* something—some possibility, some final actuality—to celebrate. "On the same night in which he was betrayed . . . he took the cup." If there could be celebration on that night, there may be celebration on any night. Unless we are able to celebrate now, no matter what the circumstances, we may never fully enjoy celebration at all. "It is truly meet, right, and salutary that we should at all times and in all places give thanks."

Celebration is, of course, valuable in itself. One does not ask when he raises a glass or sings a song, "Now what am I doing this *for?*" And yet celebration may also prove to be strangely powerful in the face of stubborn sobrieties—more powerful than customary forces and strategies alone could ever be. Paul and Silas sang in prison, and doors opened. Martyrs sang on the way to the lions, and an empire began to take up their songs. A monk sang in the face of "the old evil foe," whose might and guile he fully appreciated but whom one little word could fell, and neither the church nor very much else in the world has ever been the same since. We have heard in our own day irrepressible songs, clapping, and laughter in the face of fire hoses, police dogs, and cow prods, in paddy wagons and jails—and doors which were locked for many decades have begun to open. Red-neck rhetoric which prevailed for hundreds of years behind entrenched walls met its match only when men, women, and children began to march and sing around those walls. Protest groups are turning to less amiable forms of resistance today, but we need not altogether forget the power of clear-eyed mirth, alongside other measures, in the face of inhuman oppression.

From the celebration of the Supper we may turn expectantly to every other celebration, familiar or unfamiliar, simple or refined. There is no place or time in which one who keeps this feast is not ready to see what is to be seen and to enjoy what is to be enjoyed. There is, as we have noted, a pursuit of pleasure which depends on closing one's eyes to life—but such pleasure is no match for that which comes with a willingness to see. That very willingness is the beginning of joy, the joy which cannot be taken away. Those who have attended to the bread and wine of the Lord's Supper should be ready for all "visible words," for shaped or enacted human expressions of every sort. Those who have found forgiveness in the death of Christ should be ready for whatever is new. Frank O'Hara, the late New York artist, described such readiness as the gift within all gifts:

Grace
To be born and live as variously as possible.

Paul summoned such a response to new forms of expression in his repeated command to "rejoice in the Lord always:" "Whatever is true, whatever is honorable, whatever is just, whatever is pure, whatever is lovely, whatever is gracious, if there is any excellence, if there is anything worthy of praise, think about these things" (Phil. 4:8). One who responds in this way does not merely cling to familiar experiences; but neither does he respond to new experiences without any memory at all.

Sometimes it seems that for participants today every juice of joy and every spark of spontaneity has gone out of the Lord's Supper. Occasionally it is said that we must look for "new sacraments." Why not celebrate with other elements (say, pretzels and beer) or in other places (say, the corner tavern)? There is a certain validity in these suggestions. Paul himself pointed away from the churchly celebration to all other eating and drinking: "So, whether you eat or drink, or whatever you do, do all to the glory of God" (I Cor. 10:31). Bread and wine betoken "whatever we do"—life's most basic toils and richest pleasures. From neither sort of activity should celebration be lacking. Yet simply substituting other celebrations for the Lord's Supper seems at once too little and too much. Too little, in that without some explicit memory of the Lord's death and without the vision caught there, we are likely to seize our bread and wine or any other gift without reflection, without thanksgiving, and without the resulting quality of joy; bread and wine can be used to numb the mind as well as to quicken it. Too much, in that other meals at other places need not become weighed down with memorial or ceremonial words; there is something disruptive and even abusive about calling every good thing which all men share a "sacrament" or "form of church."

The answer, no doubt, is to see in the Lord's Supper a "hidden discipline" from which we go to all other toils and delights—a typical happening from which we go to participate in all other happenings. For those who have celebrated this death, Christ may be in every occasion, and amid every occasion they may be in Christ. If we remember that death and take this cup, we will see a new stirring in every other cup. If we take this cup and say, "I will lift up the cup of salvation and call on the name of the Lord" (Ps. 116:13), it will not be different when we offer any other toast!

NINE

A Crown Amid
Cheers and Jeering

Pilate entered the praetorium again and called Jesus, and said to him, "Are you the King of the Jews?" Jesus answered, "Do you say this of your own accord, or did others say it to you about me?" Pilate answered, "Am I a Jew? Your own nation and the chief priests have handed you over to me; what have you done?" Jesus answered, "My kingship is not of this world; if my kingship were of this world, my servants would fight, that I might not be handed over to the Jews; but my kingship is not from the world." Pilate said to him, "So you are a king?" Jesus answered, "You say that I am a king. For this I was born, and for this I have come into the world, to bear witness to the truth. Every one who is of the truth hears my voice." Pilate said to him, "What is truth?"

After he had said this, he went out to the Jews again, and told them, "I find no crime in him. But you have a custom that I should release one man for you at the Passover; will you have me release for you the King of the Jews?" They cried out again, "Not this man, but Barabbas!" Now Barabbas was a robber.

Then Pilate took Jesus and scourged him. And the soldiers plaited a crown of thorns, and put it on his head, and arrayed him in a purple robe; they came up to him, saying, "Hail, King of the Jews!" and struck him with their hands. Pilate went out again, and said to them, "Behold, I am bringing him out to you, that you may know that I find no crime in him." So Jesus came out, wearing the crown of thorns and the purple robe. Pilate said to them, "Here is the man!" When the chief priests and the officers saw him, they cried out, "Crucify him, crucify him!" Pilate said to them, "Take him yourselves and crucify him, for I find no crime in him." The

Jews answered him, "We have a law, and by that law he ought to die, because he has made himself the Son of God." When Pilate heard these words, he was the more afraid; he entered the praetorium again and said to Jesus, "Where are you from?" But Jesus gave no answer. Pilate therefore said to him, "You will not speak to me? Do you not know that I have power to release you, and power to crucify you?" Jesus answered him, "You would have no power over me unless it had been given you from above; therefore he who delivered me to you has the greater sin."

Upon this Pilate sought to release him, but the Jews cried out, "If you release this man, you are not Caesar's friend; every one who makes himself a king sets himself against Caesar." When Pilate heard these words, he brought Jesus out and sat down on the judgment seat at a place called The Pavement, and in Hebrew, Gabbatha. Now it was the day of Preparation for the Passover; it was about the sixth hour. He said to the Jews, "Here is your King!" They cried out, "Away with him, away with him, crucify him!" Pilate said to them, "Shall I crucify your King?" The chief priests answered, "We have no king but Caesar." Then he handed him over to them to be crucified.

So they took Jesus, and he went out, bearing his own cross, to the place called the place of a skull, which is called in Hebrew Golgotha. There they crucified him, and with him two others, one on either side, and Jesus between them. Pilate also wrote a title and put it on the cross; it read, "Jesus of Nazareth, the King of the Jews." Many of the Jews read this title, for the place where Jesus was crucified was near the city; and it was written in Hebrew, in Latin, and in Greek. The chief priests of the Jews then said to Pilate, "Do not write, 'The King of the Jews,' but, 'This man said, I am King of the Jews.'" Pilate answered, "What I have written I have written."

—John 18:33–19:22

*So Jesus came out, wearing the crown of thorns and the
purple robe. Pilate said to them, "Here is the man!"*—John
19:5

*Blessed is he who cometh in the Name of the Lord;
Hosanna in the highest!*—Sanctus

THE SCENES BEFORE US MAKE
up a strangely shifting combination. A cheering procession into
the city becomes, in a rapid succession of frames, a mocking
ordeal and a jeering procession out of the city to a public execution. Yet in each frame the figure of a king appears. The royal
song which is heard in the first procession is to be heard as a
valid song, as one in which even the stones could join. The
mocking which is heard in the later scenes is equally valid or
necessary or inevitable in its own way; but the image of the king
is no less present here. Indeed, the central figure is seen to be
the true king, the "king of kings," *because* he is found in both
places. Some luminous understanding, perpetually recognizable
but perpetually forgettable, must serve to unite these scenes.
Our first task is to see what that conception or recognition was
for those who first "awakened."

I

The Palm Sunday story is full of references to kingly traditions remembered by those who first told it. A new or renewed kingship is heralded and partially enacted in the streets
of Jerusalem on a festival occasion—though it is also a strange
occasion for such festivity since Herod is on the throne and
the Romans are firmly in power. Most of the crowd join in.
The Gospel of Matthew cites an oracle from one of the
prophets: "This took place to fulfil what was spoken by the
prophet, saying,

Tell the daughter of Zion,
Behold, your king is coming to you,
humble, and mounted on an ass,
and on a colt, the foal of an ass."

A mule was the customary mount for a king in the days of Israel's monarchy (not, as we might suppose, a sign of dishonor); the Gospel of Mark is careful to note that this was a new mule, the king's own, "on which no one has ever sat." Even the word "humble" serves to designate a genuine, legitimate king, since at the time of the prophet certain rites of penance or humiliation customarily preceded the anointing and enthronement (or ceremonial re-enthronement) of a king. The song sung by the people in this story is taken from a "royal psalm," which uses many images from the pageantry surrounding kingship in that earlier day. The cry is all-kingly, all-expectant: "Blessed be he who enters in the name of the Lord!" (Ps. 118:26; cf. Pss. 2, 22, 69, 86, 102, 116.)

Kingship festivals were familiar in the Egyptian and Mesopotamian world during the time of Israel's kings, both at the accession of a new king and at annual festivals which renewed the kingship. There is considerable evidence, especially in the psalms, that Israel had such festivals of its own. Certain basic ideas attending ancient Near Eastern kingship and its ceremonies were clearly present in Israel. The interdependence of the "righteousness" of the king and the "righteousness" of the people, as well as of the "sin" of the king and the "sin" of the people, provides a central theme of the Books of the Kings. The court chronicle in II Samuel recounts David's reign in terms of the king's ceremony, beginning with the prophet Nathan's announcement concerning David's royal house, and even including events of penance and humiliation in which the king became the vicarious bearer of all the sufferings which befell his people, and laid his dignity at the feet of the Lord to receive it again at the Lord's hand. Recall the haunting scene in which David, during the conspiracy of Absalom, leaves the city of Jerusalem, crosses the brook Kidron, and climbs the Mount of Olives, walking barefoot with his head covered, weeping as he goes, accepting the stones, curses, and mockery flung at him along the way by a scoffer from the house of Saul. When his followers wish to draw their swords, the king says, "What have I to do with you? . . . Let

116

him alone and let him curse; for the Lord has bidden him. It may be that the Lord will look upon my affliction . . ." (II Sam. 15:23–16:14). The Hebrew word for "my affliction" is the very word used again and again in the Old Testament for "the poor of the Lord," for those who truly "waited on the Lord."

Do we begin to see the kind of memory and strange recognition which stirred in those who first told the stories of Palm Sunday and the passion? The royal psalms had preserved many images from the kingship ceremony: the king seated on his royal mule; the procession through "the gates of righteousness" to the anointing in the temple and the enthronement in the palace; the cry "Hosanna"—"Save us;" the king standing on a high platform in full view of the people with the crown on his head and the purple robe on his shoulders; the climax coming with the announcement that this was the true son of David who rules at the right hand of Jahweh, with respect to whom all other kings are advised to "be wise." But how could such images and ceremonies of kingship ever become attached to someone who was rejected by the chief priests and rulers, scorned by the people, and executed by the powers of his day? Now the stirring begins: were there not also those rites of expiation which the king had to endure while he prayed for healing and salvation in the people? Thus, the king cries in the psalm: "All nations surrounded me. . . . They surrounded me like bees, they blazed like a fire of thorns. . . . I was pushed hard, so that I was falling" (Ps. 118:10–13; cf. Ps. 22: 12–21). In a sixth-century B.C. ritual which has come to us from Babylon, the king was actually slapped and spat upon, and hairs were plucked from his cheek while the people mocked and wagged their heads, playing the parts of their national enemies. More stirring: was there not also that great song about the servant-king, coming out of reflection on the exile in Babylon and pointing to a new calling for a new Israel: "He was despised and rejected by men; a man of sorrows, and acquainted with grief. . . . We esteemed him stricken, smitten by God, and afflicted. . . . He was oppressed and he

117

was afflicted, yet he opened not his mouth" (Isa. 53; cf. Isa. 50:6). To be sure, such suffering for others had seldom, if ever, been identified with the Davidic Messiah who was to come. Like other kings, the Messiah might suffer a temporary setback, but there was little thought that his suffering was the very purpose of his coming. That was the new thing— such a new thing that the reader is required to catch at that new significance for himself in scene after scene of the passion story.

"So you are a king?" Pilate asks Jesus in the Fourth Gospel. You who stand before me unattended, bound, stripped, condemned, bruised, you who fled when the crowds attempted to make you their king and yet deliberately entered the city in a ceremonial procession—you are a king? From that beaten figure comes a strange reply. Though Pilate had gotten his question from others who rejected the idea, he himself had said the words: Jesus was a king. "For this was I born, and for this I have come into the world, to bear witness to the truth. Every one who is of the truth hears my voice." The Roman procurator is accustomed to asking more palpable questions concerning power, but he pauses long enough to pose the question which seemed in search of a voice: "What is truth?" The word for truth in the Greek text literally means an "unveiling." In the question of kingship passing between Pilate and Jesus something is waiting to be revealed.

Now Jesus stands on the platform in plain view of the people, slapped, mocked, wearing the crown of thorns and the purple robe. He is pronounced innocent by Pilate, who also makes two other announcements to the people: "Here is the man!" and (sitting now in the judgment seat) "Here is your King!" But the people call for crucifixion. There is a certain necessity that one in whom kingship and truth are found should be mocked, and a certain necessity that one who is truly man should be crucified—both by and for the people.

Now the time has come for the enthronement. The procession leads not to a palace but to a mound called the place of a skull. The crown is a wreath of thorns; the royal crimson is the king's own blood; the throne is a cross; the courtiers are thieves. The moment has arrived for the ceremonial announcement. When the crowd looks up at the man thus enthroned, it sees an official inscription on the cross: "Jesus of Nazareth, the King of the Jews." The title is written in three languages, at least one of which is known to every man or woman who passes by—all nations could read it and be warned. The chief priests rush back to Pilate, disowning this king, arguing that Jesus was only a pretender. The procurator cuts them short with his final words in the Gospel, "What I have written I have written." It would stand. The kingship of Jesus would continue to be announced in the language of the marketplace, of religion, and of the scholar. Always, in all these places, there are some who are strangely stirred and awakened, for whom this king is vindicated and raised up by God himself.

II

We ourselves do not have the same remembrance of kingship or kingship ceremonies which helped to characterize those who first responded to Jesus and to these luminous accounts of his passion and death. We do, however, still speak of power, of differing and successive forms of power within political, military, industrial, economic, and social systems. Every form of power has its own dynamic or manner of working and depends for its effectiveness on material conditions and human purposes at a particular time and place. It functions until it is overtaken by a newer, more applicable or more equitable form of power. "Power corrupts," if not through "moral" corruption then through the corruptions of time and change. It is no less necessary for that. We use and enjoy it while it lasts. But, as with the kings of old, our forms of power rise and fall; they have their day and yield to a successor.

What seems to be required is a willingness to use power *and* a certain willingness to relinquish it. A society is imperiled (especially in a time of amassed power and rapid change) when outworn institutions do not die gracefully—though that is rare in human affairs. We do not expect any form of power to yield without a struggle. Timing is often the issue, since the old must hold on to its functions until it is fully replaced by the new, lest a power vacuum develop and chaos ensue. There is, moreover, a kind of humiliation in letting go of power, in putting off a former adulation or respect. Yet in a combination of exercising power and putting off power there is truth. This touches at what was seen in Jesus, and what is still seen by those who call him "Lord" or "King." But those who do so still "follow afar off" and are, at best, only "unprofitable servants" of this king.

What would it mean to be a follower of this "Lord" or "King" amid the realities of power today? It would mean recognizing from the outset that one's own exercise of power in whatever calling or agency has only a limited validity, that it does not solve every human problem, and that it will not always provide the best solution to the kind of problem it addresses. On the basis of this understanding, a faithful man might more readily alter his services or professional regulations to meet the realities of a new day. He might urge his industry to retool or even to alter its forms of management and control, in response to changes taking place in the society. But present power and profit often stand in the way, causing delay long after the hour has come to change. Where men think primarily in terms of accustomed or congenial conceptions, where they explicitly ask immediate questions of power and only implicitly ask further questions of truth, a certain reluctance is to be expected. Where this is the case, there is a certain kingship in accepting some mocking, no less than that found in accepting praise.

Following this "King" would also mean new focus and organization at places in the society where power is lacking. There are many uncrowned heads which need to know their power and authority as men. As the powerful need to learn an appropriate "humiliation" or limitation, the humiliated need to learn their proper power. Both of these actions are sung in the *Magnificat:* "He has put down the mighty from their thrones, and exalted those of low degree" (Luke 1:52). Helping those of low degree to claim their crowns requires something more than gifts of charity or welfare. To give charity is still to exercise lordship; it is still not helping men to "reign." "The kings of the Gentiles exercise lordship over them; and those in authority over them are called benefactors," Jesus says for the benefit of all would-be benefactors, ". . . but I am among you as one who serves" (Luke 22:25–27). To give aid to the previously exploited as an act of justice, and to allow the use of such "reparations" for the establishment of new seats of power and function, may help to raise men up. Those who serve the kingship of other men in these ways may expect to bear humiliation and mockery from others who wish only to give charity, and perhaps even from those who wish only to receive it.

"Here is the man!" "Here is your King!" The one of whom these proclamations were made was not a professional or political king, yet he was seen to truly wear a crown. His true crown—a crown of truth—was not given by any institution in the world, either in praise or jest; he came wearing a crown into the world by virtue of his human birth. Those who saw him as king saw the world raised up, ruled, "upheld" by his power. They sang a new song of one who, having come on the scene as a man, "humbled himself and became obedient unto death, even death on a cross" in the service of the manhood of others, and who for that very reason is called "the Lord" (Phil. 2:5–11). Still the song goes up, "King of kings and Lord of lords," "he shall reign for ever and ever" (Rev. 19:16; 22:5). That song is not a wish or a dream or a sentimental theme song. It is an affirmation of brute and glorious reality, present in germ and still to come, which may be scorned or praised but which is not finally to be denied.

III

"Blessed is he who cometh in the Name of the Lord." We have read these words not only from the psalm and from the Gospel but from the liturgy, which sets modern people down amid those ancient scenes and in which they make these words their own. We have reasons, both old and new, to reflect before we sing them again. These words are sung not about one who merely speaks the name of the Lord or teaches the name

121

of the Lord; they are not about one who merely reads or writes the name of the Lord. They are about one who *comes* in the name of the Lord. There is a warning in this for all who ever use or take the name of the Lord. A man who does not take the name of the Lord at all may at least be said not to blaspheme it; and he may yet be brought to the vision and obedience of faith. But what can be done with the man who takes the name of the Lord in vain?

There are two ways of taking that name in vain. The first is to take the name of the Lord without taking up the Lord's load, the yoke and burden of Jesus Christ in the world which crucified him. There are references to the Lord, and words about the doctrines of faith, which appear to grow legs and go all by themselves—making little reference either to the Bible *or* to the newspaper. Everyone has smiled at the theologian who spends so much time talking about the Lord that he forgets to say any prayers or to sing any songs at all—or so much time praying and singing to the Lord that he forgets to get on with the answer and the action. To "come in the name of the Lord" *means* to "get on with it." That is required not only to communicate faith, but even to hold it.

Another way to take the Lord's name in vain is to take up the Lord's name, and even something of the Lord's load, without taking up the Lord's song. In bearing the load that was waiting to be borne, in doing so for other men who did not see it or take it up, Jesus was seen as "true man" and the world was seen as becoming through him "true world." There is no vision or discovery to compare with that. That is why Jesus could recommend his yoke to other men. "For my yoke is easy, and my burden is light" (Matt. 11:29 f.). That is why he sang a hymn with his disciples before going out into the night. To be a man in the world, to be for the world in the way of Christ, to know oneself and the world together in that way—that is worth a song, even if one finds himself the only singer! To take the Lord's name without taking up the Lord's load is empty. To take up the Lord's load without the Lord's song is blind.

It is also dangerous. We have all met men and women who think of themselves joylessly as "suffering for others" or "sacrificing themselves for others." They have our thanks—preferably in writing. "Sacrifice" and "suffering" are dangerous words. One who suffers is always in danger of becoming sentimental about himself—in which case (as in being "sorry for Jesus") he misses the very point of Christ. One who makes some sacrifice is always in danger of becoming uncritical of himself and unduly critical of others. He imagines his sufferings to be identical with those of Christ, to be exactly the kind which uphold the world. His own programs then become a new law, not really discussable. The name, the vision, and the song are lost. In their place are self-importance, the fixed idea, and a long face—these have their reward. Even the amusement they provoke in less scrupulous men seems deserving.

There was a time when Christians sought to clarify their faith by asking themselves the paradigmatic question, What is the difference, if any, between Socrates and Christ, between the hemlock and the cross? Today the question is somewhat altered: What is the difference, they are asking, between Sisyphus and Christ—the former rolling his stone up the hill against time and death, against breeding microbes and speeding traffic, in the face of economic change and delicate political balances, without alternative or rest or hope; the latter carrying his cross up the same hill against the same obstacles "in the name of the Lord," "for the joy that is set before him"? It is there, on a thousand hills, between those who roll the stone and those who bear the cross, that the most significant "dialogues" of our day are taking place. It is there, on those very hills, that it takes place within ourselves.

The difference lies not in taking up the load, but in taking up the load with a song—because there *is* a song waiting to be sung, and because somebody has to sing it for the stones!

TEN

Has It Ever Dawned on You?

Now on the first day of the week Mary Magdalene came to the tomb early, while it was still dark, and saw that the stone had been taken away from the tomb. So she ran, and went to Simon Peter and the other disciple, the one whom Jesus loved, and said to them, "They have taken the Lord out of the tomb, and we do not know where they have laid him." Peter then came out with the other disciple, and they went toward the tomb. They both ran, but the other disciple outran Peter and reached the tomb first; and stooping to look in, he saw the linen cloths lying there, but he did not go in. Then Simon Peter came, following him, and he went into the tomb; he saw the linen cloths lying, and the napkin, which had been on his head, not lying with the linen cloths but rolled up in a place by itself. Then the other disciple, who reached the tomb first, also went in, and he saw and believed; for as yet they did not know the scripture, that he must rise from the dead. Then the disciples went back to their homes.

But Mary stood weeping outside the tomb, and as she wept she stooped to look into the tomb; and she saw two angels in white, sitting where the body of Jesus had lain, one at the head and one at the feet. They said to her, "Woman, why are you weeping?" She said to them, "Because they have taken away my Lord, and I do not know where they have laid him." Saying this, she turned round and saw Jesus standing, but she did not know that it was Jesus. Jesus said to her, "Woman, why are you weeping? Whom do you seek?" Supposing him to be the gardener, she said to him, "Sir, if you have carried him away, tell me where you have laid him,

*and I will take him away." Jesus said to her, "Mary." She turned
and said to him in Hebrew, "Rabboni!" (which means Teacher).
Jesus said to her, "Do not hold me, for I have not yet ascended to
the Father; but go to my brethren and say to them, I am ascending
to my Father and your Father, to my God and your God." Mary
Magdalene went and said to the disciples, "I have seen the Lord";
and she told them that he had said these things to her.*

*On the evening of that day, the first day of the week, the doors
being shut where the disciples were, for fear of the Jews, Jesus
came and stood among them and said to them, "Peace be with you."
When he had said this, he showed them his hands and his side.
Then the disciples were glad when they saw the Lord. Jesus said
to them again, "Peace be with you. As the Father has sent me,
even so I send you." And when he had said this, he breathed on
them, and said to them, "Receive the Holy Spirit. If you forgive
the sins of any, they are forgiven; if you retain the sins of any,
they are retained."*

*Now Thomas, one of the twelve, called the Twin, was not with
them when Jesus came. So the other disciples told him, "We have
seen the Lord." But he said to them, "Unless I see in his hands
the print of the nails, and place my hand in his side, I will not
believe."*

*Eight days later, his disciples were again in the house, and Thomas
was with them. The doors were shut, but Jesus came and stood
among them, and said, "Peace be with you." Then he said to
Thomas, "Put your finger here, and see my hands; and put out
your hand, and place it in my side; do not be faithless, but believing."
Thomas answered him, "My Lord and my God!" Jesus said to him
"Have you believed because you have seen me? Blessed are those
who have not seen and yet believe."*

*Now Jesus did many other signs in the presence of the disciples,
which are not written in this book; but these are written that you
may believe that Jesus is the Christ, the Son of God, and that believing you may have life in his name.*

—John 20

Have you believed because you have seen me? Blessed are those who have not seen and yet believe.—John 20:29

The peace of the Lord be with you always.—Pax Domini

THE FIRST STORIES OF EASTER, and our first celebrations, are set at dawn. There are few better words than "dawn" for describing the discovery or disclosure or (to use a third term which refers both to what happens and to our grasp of that happening) the truth which we remember and celebrate today. Dawn is the moment of passage from darkness to light everywhere in the world each day. Yet it would be pointless to speak of any passage from darkness to light except by reference to some creature which is able to see and rejoice in that light. To contemplate that connection between what is or what happens and its being seen or understood is to think about the *kind* of mystery or solemnity Easter celebrates.

For no Gospel is the "dawning" character of Easter more explicit than the one we read today. The Fourth Gospel has spoken from the outset about "darkness" and "light," about the light coming to darkness and the darkness not overcoming it (or not "comprehending" it), about a light coming into the world which must enlighten every man (John 1:4 9). Here at the very end it is still talking about darkness and light and about coming from darkness to light. The resurrection stories which it recounts begin in darkness and proceed from one kind of seeing to another, toward an intended kind of seeing which should be distinguished from the first kind and which may even be separate from it—at least so far as our own seeing is concerned.

There are certain features of the Easter lessons which bother us, and it may be well for us to admit that from the start. At each mention of angels, or of a sudden appearance of Jesus and a just as sudden disappearance, we are likely to cringe a little or to play with our gloves. If these items do not put us off on Easter Day, they are sufficiently problematic to help us put the whole thing aside on the days which follow. Possibly

127

these elements in the Easter lessons do not cause us any embarrassment or surprise at all. But in that case we might be missing something of their intended purpose—if there was a point in their very oddness and in the resulting surprise.

If anything is clear from the outset, it is that surprise was written right into these stories. The point is not merely that they seem surprising to *us* who live in a more technical, less credulous age. The Gospel of Mark, which may be the earliest Gospel, ends abruptly in a tremor of surprise and silence: "They went out and fled from the tomb; for trembling and astonishment had come upon them; and they said nothing to any one, for they were afraid" (16:8). That's where it leaves us, and that's how it *means* to leave us (though a sequel was added in later editions). We are meant to be left squirming with something which is trying to break through to us, in an attitude of awe and attention and discovery—an awe heightened for the first readers by the fact that the phrase "He has risen" referred to the end of the age, to a future resurrected kingdom. What could it mean to say that Jesus belonged to *that,* or that *that* had somehow already begun?

The angels in the Gospel stories of the resurrection are not merely there to remind us that certain first-century people believed in angels and that we should try to believe in them too. They are not merely there to tell us that a man who was dead walked again and that we should try to believe that we too will live again after we die—as an additional fact now simply added to the facts we already know. Such information or exhortation may indeed have seemed less surprising to the first tellers of these stories than it seems to us. The angels are there in those stories to signal something as surprising for the first tellers as it is for us: that "this Jesus who was crucified" was a source of light and not of darkness, and that henceforth they were to see all things in a new and dazzling light! Here at the end of our chapter of Easter lessons the point is made for all later readers: we are to "see" all things in a new light, even if we have not "seen" the particular things reported by the first disciples.

128

I

When Mary Magdalene comes to the tomb at the outset of our Easter story, it is still dark. The garden—the whole world —is dark and she can see only that the stone has been taken away. She draws the simplest and most direct inference to be made on the basis of that kind of evidence: the body had been stolen. That is the word she carries back to Peter and "the other disciple."

The story of the two disciples is told next, and here we learn to distinguish some further kinds of seeing. (Three different words are used for "seeing" in this text, referring somewhat successively to sight, scrutiny, and insight.) The other disciple outruns Peter and reaches the tomb first; he stoops and looks into the tomb only slightly more intently than Mary had done. Peter comes up, goes right into the tomb, and begins to inspect the grave clothes, examining and weighing the evidence. Then the first disciple enters and, apparently without extended scrutiny, believes! It is not said whether Peter, for all his sifting of the evidence, came to *that* kind of seeing-and-believing at this time or not. The nameless disciple, who saw the least evidence, "saw" the most by faith. Peter, the "name" disciple, who saw the most evidence, is not said to have "seen" anything by faith. Neither of these disciples, moreover, took any new or surprising action on the basis of what he had seen. Both simply "went back to their own homes"—as everyone did at the end of the crucifixion—exemplifying a prophecy of Zechariah in which the whole land mourned, "each family by itself" (12:10–14). The disciple who saw the light did not yet talk or walk as in the day—as Mary, who was not one of the twelve and who was a woman besides, *would* do. The point to be noted, surely, is that the light in question does not come simply on the basis of status or study or virtue; this light (even more notably than light in other matters) is "turned on" or "given."

Now we are back with Mary in the garden. She has "seen" the open tomb but she is still weeping. She stoops to look into the tomb more closely, still not seeing, not letting herself see, not admitting to herself what she sees—like someone on "Candid Camera" who finds herself in strange circumstances but does not dare to show anything but a poker face. The angels are there for Mary, the message is waiting to break through to her, but she persists in seeing things only as she has seen them before. Why is she weeping? Because they have taken away her Lord and she does not know where they have laid him. The risen Lord himself speaks to her, but she refuses to hear anything in other than an accustomed way. What is to be expected in a garden but a gardener? "Sir, if you have carried him away, tell me where you have laid him, and I will take him away." Everything is straining to say that there is more here than meets the eye, and that what meets the eye does not all by itself bring the desired understanding.

That undertsanding occurs when Jesus speaks the one, personal name "Mary"—not "woman" but "Mary." All at once the "dawn" breaks, darkness and sorrow flee, the world lights up. What was it about that proper name—the remembrance of things past, of a personal joy in the company of Jesus which had meant more to her than she had ever admitted even to herself, of a secret hope hidden beneath her sorrow? Was happiness always marred by sorrow for oneself? Did that name now speak to an inner life heretofore locked up against the world? Was it a sense of "being known" better than she knew herself, of having a home in the world after all? Was her passion not so displaced or fortuitous as it had seemed— so that now she could step out of her isolation as a detached, suspicious, defensive visitor, and become an engaged participant in the world? Had this question been stirring within her, scarcely recognized, even repressed, until at last she heard her own name, "Mary"? Is it only *after* their eyes are opened that men admit to themselves and to one another that their hearts have been burning within them along the road . . . ?

All seeing is a private matter; no one can ever see for anyone else, even in the simplest sense of seeing. What is seen can be shared or compared only through speech. In larger senses of "seeing"—seeing what is good or right or to be undertaken in the world—it is even more a matter of each for himself, at least so far as gaining agreement is concerned. It is no wonder that what is seen in that way seems a private matter, and potentially illusory if we assign it a public or objective significance. But the word to Mary from Jesus does not merely chide wishful illusions; it also gently mocks the notion that sentiments and commitments are simply adrift in the world, not belonging to it at all—"Mary!" Did not her passions and commitments have consequences beyond herself and beyond the people who shared them? How could they be merely wishful if they imposed costly demands which might require her very life, and if they were both recognized and disciplined by Christ? Mary responds not with the common noun "gardener" but with "Rabboni!"—"my teacher," one who puts things together for me, one who enlightens me!

The next words are puzzling: "Do not hold me, for I have not yet ascended . . . to my Father and your Father, to my God and your God." Are they meant to warn Mary (and us) that as ordinary physical seeing had not in itself produced her new faith, neither should she expect to have Jesus in the ordinary ways of seeing and touching? As her faith was not merely wishful, neither would its responses be; she would henceforth walk in the light as he had done. From now on she would see and touch all other things in a new way.

II

It is dark again on the evening of that day, but nowhere is it darker than in the room where the doors are shut and the disciples are huddled together for fear of the Jews. Once again the story proceeds by steps of sight to insight. Jesus "showed them his hands and his side"—the light, when it came, would refer not to a different world but to the very world they had shared with him, the one in which he had been crucified. "Then the disciples were glad when they saw the Lord."

This illumination and joy were not given on the basis of any special virtue within the recipients. The disciples were not, in the stories they themselves and their followers told, unusually wise, good, or courageous men. They were a bunch of sagging knees and crumpled hearts when the light dawned around them. The Easter stories are always upbraiding them for their unbelief or calling them "foolish men, and slow of heart to believe." Lest this point escape us, the greatest utterance of faith is reserved for that disciple who is the most deeply disaffected; the most doubting becomes the most confessing. In view of the cruelties of the past days, Thomas had made it a policy not accept anything as real or true except on the evidence or "verification" of his senses. He had adopted his warrants: he would have to see and touch the very wounds which for him now seemed the final facts of life. But when he is invited to touch and see, he comes to "see" much more than could ever be an object of sight or touch: "My Lord and my God!"

When, earlier in the chapter, Mary and the disciples said "We have seen the Lord," they need hardly have meant more than "the Master"—the one they knew and followed together before he died. Here in the speech of Thomas the word "Lord" contains almost unmistakably the full faithful reflection of the New Testament believers on Jesus as *kurios*, the one in whom they had "seen the Father." This confession is spoken by one who, by his previous lights, had found no reason whatever to believe. His confession is not simply given "by flesh and blood," nor can any credit be claimed for it by flesh and blood. Yet *what* he confesses is full of significance for his flesh and blood—for the future of Thomas, the traveler and martyr.

Even this is not quite the closing point. There is a confession even more appropriate than that of the disciples and Thomas, one which is the curtain-dropper not only of this chapter but of the entire Gospel. "Have you believed because you have seen me? Blessed are those who have not seen and yet believe." The word "blessed" is still passive. That is how faith has described itself before the gift of light in every age. On this note the Gospel ends. Many other signs were given—there is a world full of witness—but these were written to be the occasion of faith and new life in many others who do not see the same sights but who may come to stand in the same light.

III

Let us stay for a moment with this picture of Christ standing among the disciples. We have seen that the "light" of which Easter speaks must "come on" for every man within himself. Yet *what* it illumines is, also, the common life. Words used to designate the most distinctive human characteristics usually refer to situations in which there are two or more people. Words like "good," "loving," and "noble" refer not to the way a man is all by himself but rather to how he is with others. Similarly, in this picture, Christ does not come to each disciple separately, making him into a good or brave man first and then sending him to others. The disciples are all together in a single room when Jesus comes and stands among them and says to them, "Peace be with you." He breathes on them together and says, "Receive the Holy Spirit. If you forgive the sins of any, they are forgiven."

There is a form of forgiveness which, while familiar, is undynamic. As we expect to defend ourselves against one another, we may also expect to indulge one another that we may be indulged. Such forgiveness amounts to a conspiracy against change or development in ourselves and others. The forgiveness authorized by the risen Lord, when it appears, is different. The forgiven and the forgiving now refer to a demand made upon them which is not simply imposed by one upon the other or by common agreement, but which needs to be accepted by both. Being together as modest and free men, neither coercing nor indulging one another, is not only a picture but a permanent possibility through Christ. Christ still appears as a surprising basis of human community. Easter may dawn and shed its light not only on matters of personal sorrow but on every meeting between man and man.

We all know what we have to do in order to get along socially, to achieve status, or even (as we say) to make love. There are "how to" manuals on all these matters; there is even a new science of "human engineering." Nothing in our lessons should make us less industrious in acquiring such skills; but those lessons also point to ends which govern the use of those skills. In loving, one has to pay attention to the object of his affection, not merely to his own feeling or display of affection. A full relationship depends, moreover, on a similar motion from the other side. A man can do many things for his son, but he can't be a real father to his son unless his son is willing to let him be one, unless the son is willing to be a son toward his father. Each must let go of himself to be for the other— and each receives himself back from the other. It should be added that *what* we must wish for another person is his *proper* good, not merely one which seems most agreeable or convenient to ourselves, and not merely one he happens to wish for himself. What we wish for one another, and enjoy together in every faithful relationship, is Christ! Now do we see something of the light which the Crucified One sheds on all societal life? "Whoever would save his life will lose it," Jesus says in all four Gospels, "and whoever loses his life for my sake and the gospel's will save it" (Mark 8:35; Matt. 10:39; Luke 17:33; John 12:25).

This, of course, is not science or social science in the technical sense. It is the very point of these stories that the light of which they speak is not itself a human achievement. But once it comes, will this light not also shine on *what* is studied and help to show what is to be *done* with what is learned? To be sure, it does not alter the facts concerning race, housing, unemployment, education, or political conflicts; but will not such facts be viewed with a new intensity if they all refer to "brethren for whom Christ died"? Will that light not search out needs we might otherwise have overlooked or have heretofore been unwilling to see? Beyond the needs of men for charity, their needs for equity? Beyond their needs for equity, their needs for active participation? Even that is not the end

if, in this light, we see all other men as having private sentiments and individual vitalities which need to find expression
in the light of day.

IV

Some of us are no doubt itching to say that this is all very
interesting but we have never understood Easter in this way,
that we ourselves have never seen this light, that we need more
evidence that this is so or more guidance in finding out that
it is so. Such questions are never far from any of us, but we
must be very careful in answering them. The stories themselves
warn against seeking evidence of a technical sort for the
perspective or conviction of Easter. One does not come to faith
simply on the basis of argument or evidence; nor for that
matter does one lose his faith in that way. One can admit the
cross and an empty tomb, one can even believe the witnesses
who said they saw the Lord, without receiving all the Gospels
mean to impart. When one "falls from faith," it is less appropriate to say that his faith has been "disproved" than to say
simply that his faith has been "lost." The light which once
dawned now seems withdrawn; the world grows dark again as
before the dawn. It becomes a place of tombs and gardeners,
of evidence without witness, of crosses without joy.

One cannot command the light or say to the dawn, "Be
soon." But one can stand in places where the light is said to
shine or where the witness is made. That would include those
places in the world where luminous actions are needed and
taken. The Fourth Gospel speaks of a witness to Christ in
"worldly" places; the woman at the well in Samaria, the official
in the streets of Capernaum, and Pontius Pilate in the judgment
hall, all in their way bear witness. Something of Christ may be
seen in scientific study which not only seeks to extract the
secrets of the earth but also takes delight in them; in political
actions and social movements which seem most free to seek a
better city—as though freedom and hope have a place in the
objective world; in theater and games which pursue our last

pretension or in music which plays in the very presence of guilt and fear. If we find ourselves believing that knowledge is more than power, that good is more than preference, that love is more than sentiment, that joy is more than pleasure—we may actually be seeing in this light. We need only start walking in that light.

Or we may come to stand not only among the half-believing unbelievers in all those places, but also among the half-unbelieving believers of the church. Here the name itself is spoken. Here the story is duly told. Here the death of Jesus is regularly set forth in bread and wine and all must play their roles as crucifiers, witless bystanders, or men both crucified and reconstituted through him. The "peace of the Lord" is still announced, forgiveness is enacted, the Spirit is celebrated, and obedience is specified for the present moment. Men are still "sent" to be in the world as he was "sent." We need not be entirely put off by uneven responses from the people who wait in this place. The light is something which comes; it is not something for which men qualify. Yet if Mary had never wandered back to the garden, if the disciples had not gathered again in the upper room, if the two along the road had not been ruminating on the Scriptures and dwelling on the story of Christ—what would have dawned on them then? How would they have recognized the light when it shined? It is possible to walk that road every day of one's life in the light of life, looking for nothing more than the ice-cream man—and finding nothing more. It is one of the perplexities of the Easter gospel stories that the risen Christ appeared only to those who had been disciples—and it is one of their abiding truths.

A final clue to the matter is this. If the light is hard to see, the reason may not be that it is too far away but that it is too near. While we are standing and seeing in the light, we do not see the light itself. Christ is closer to us than sight, closer than touch, closer than our self-understanding or our chosen pursuits. "Do not say in your heart, 'Who will ascend into heaven?' (that is, to bring Christ down) or 'Who will descend into the abyss?' (that is, to bring Christ up from the dead). . . . The word is near you, on your lips and in your heart" (Rom. 10:6–). He stands among us. All the time we are foolishly and studiously seeking him, he is patiently—or impatiently—waiting for us. When the light finally dawns it is not really an extraordinary or supernatural event at all. It is the most natural event of all.

For all who have been squinting, huddling, and adopting policies along the way, there are fellow-travelers in the stumbling disciples of these stories. To all who have been "sleeping for sorrow" the light of another day comes to say, "Has it ever dawned on you?"

THE PREACHER'S PAPERBACK LIBRARY

Volumes already published:

1. *The Servant of the Word* by H. H. Farmer. 1964.
2. *The Care of the Earth and Other University Sermons* by Joseph Sittler. 1964.
3. *The Preaching of F. W. Robertson* edited with an Introduction by Gilbert E. Doan, Jr. 1964.
4. *A Brief History of Preaching* by Yngve Brilioth. 1965.
5. *The Living Word* by Gustaf Wingren. 1965.
6. *On Prayer* by Gerhard Ebeling. 1966.
7. *Renewal in the Pulpit*—Sermons by Younger Preachers edited with an Introduction by Edmund A. Steimle. 1966.
8. *The Preaching of Chrysostom: Homilies on the Sermon on the Mount* edited with an Introduction by Jaroslav Pelikan. 1967.
9. *Violent Sleep*—Notes Toward the Development of Sermons in the Modern City by Richard Luecke. 1969.

Type, 10 on 11 Garamond and 9 on 10 Granjon.
Display, Garamond.